KIDNAPPED
AND OTHER DISPATCHES

ALAN JOHNSTON

Edited by Tony Grant

P
PROFILE BOOKS

First published in Great Britain in 2007 by
PROFILE BOOKS LTD
3A Exmouth House
Pine Street
London EC1R 0JH
www.profilebooks.com

10 9 8 7 6 5 4 3 2 1

Typeset in Quadraat by MacGuru Ltd
info@macguru.org.uk
Printed and bound in Great Britain by Clays, Bungay, Suffolk

ISBN 978 1 84668 142 4

The paper this book is printed on is certified by the © 1996 Forest
Stewardship Council A.C. (FSC). It is ancient-forest friendly. The printer
holds FSC chain of custody SGS-COC-2061

FSC
Mixed Sources
Product group from well-managed
forests and other controlled sources

Cert no. SGS-COC-2061
www.fsc.org
© 1996 Forest Stewardship Council

KIDNAPPED

Alan Johnston was born in Lindi, Tanzania. He studied English and politics at Dundee University and joined the BBC in 1991. In 1993 he became the BBC's correspondent in Central Asia and later in Afghanistan. His three-year posting in Gaza began in April 2004 and was due to finish days after his capture. Since his release he has returned to Scotland to be with his immediate family.

Tony Grant, the editor of this book, has been the producer of *From Our Own Correspondent* for the last fifteen years. He joined the BBC after working in commercial radio and newspapers in Merseyside.

To my family and everyone at the BBC and beyond who campaigned so hard for my release when I was kidnapped in Gaza, and for reporters anywhere in the world who are persecuted or imprisoned for their journalism.

CONTENTS

CENTRAL ASIA

Foreword

From Our Own Correspondent has been on the air for more than fifty years, helping listeners to BBC Radio make more sense of what's going on in other parts of the world. It offers them a direct personal link to the BBC's army of correspondents and a chance to share the enthusiasm they feel in covering what are often momentous events in exotic locations.

In a world where a story must often be condensed into a minute or less, or perhaps confined to a single answer to a programme presenter's question, *From Our Own Correspondent* provides correspondents with an opportunity to say a little more: to provide some of the context to the stories they're covering, to describe some of the characters involved and some of the sights they see as they watch events unfold.

Alan Johnston hoped, while he was being held captive in Gaza, that he would one day tell his story on *From Our Own Correspondent*, his favourite programme. That despatch, along with others he sent from earlier

postings in Afghanistan and Central Asia, can be
found within these pages.

Tony Grant
Producer
From Our Own Correspondent
Bush House
London
November 2007

THE MIDDLE
EAST

Introduction

Perhaps few places on earth have seen more violence than Gaza. It sits on an important corner of the Mediterranean, and for thousands of years it has caught the eye of conquerors. The armies of the pharaohs of ancient Egypt fought for it. So did Alexander the Great. And later the Crusader King, Richard the Lion Heart, the great Muslim warrior Salahuddin and even Napoleon Bonaparte marched through. The Greeks, the Romans, the Jews, the Turks, the British and others have all left traces of their presence in Gaza's sands. But of course it has not only been a place of many battles. Down the centuries there have been calmer spells, when Gaza has been at peace and even prospered, and it may well do so again. But I was there in one of its darker times.

In the tiny, claustrophobic sliver of land that is the Gaza Strip, the Israeli-Palestinian conflict hangs in the air you breathe. On the crowded streets, the graffiti scrawled on almost every wall is in the language of war. There are calls to arms, and the slogans of the numerous Palestinian jihadi brigades and militias – along with the names of their dead. Pretty much every day furious funeral processions carve their way through the honking chaos of the traffic, and speakers rage at political rallies. And everywhere there are green, yellow and black flags, the battle standards of Hamas, Fatah and Islamic Jihad.

There is an almost overwhelming intensity to Gaza and to be honest, at first, I was a little scared of the place. Within days of my arriving back in the summer of 2004, Israeli tanks punched hard into the city. They had come looking for the garages and workshops where rockets were made before being fired at the homes of the Jewish families in nearby, illegally built settlements. There was savage fighting. For days the city echoed to machine-gun fire, ambulances went screaming through the streets and helicopter gunships clattered overhead. There were many Palestinian dead and injured – numerous civilians among them. But several Israeli soldiers were killed too, and their body parts were taken as trophies. The word was that a militant on a motorbike was riding around showing off a severed head. And on the night when the Israelis finally pulled out, I remember a young Palestinian coming up to me in the darkness and the wreckage carrying on a stick what looked like a piece of burnt flesh. 'This,' he said, 'is from a Jew.'

And so, with that grim introduction, I began what were the three most extraordinary years of my life. Every few days there were stunning acts of violence from one side or the other. Some of what I witnessed I will never be able to shake from my mind, such as the way the sun caught the great gleaming slick of blood when a Palestinian boy was ripped in half by a tank shell in Jabalia.

And all the time the big picture was changing. Early on, the man they called Mr Palestine, Yasser Arafat, died. His people will argue over the good and the bad in his legacy for generations to come. But in Gaza, on the day they heard of his death, nobody spoke ill of Arafat. So many fires were lit on the roads in his honour that the thickest, darkest cloud I ever saw settled on the grieving city.

Halfway through my time there, the Israelis gave up their effort to colonise Gaza. They pulled out their settlers and demolished their fortified homes, built in breach of international law on occupied land. And the world looked on as Palestinian looters moved in and smashed the synagogues that the Jews had left standing in the sand dunes.

Meanwhile I watched the rise and rise of the Hamas movement. The Israelis struck repeatedly, assassinating key figures, but Hamas kept coming.

First it won a huge election victory and later routed its Fatah rivals militarily, and took complete control of Gaza. Hamas's charter calls for the destruction of the state of Israel, and its followers dream that one day – perhaps only in centuries to come, but one day – Israel will somehow be swept away, and cities like Jaffa will again be in Arab hands. And so, as I write, the West treats Hamas as a diplomatic pariah. It argues that to engage with it in any way and explore its offer of a protracted ceasefire would be to appease an organisation that has in the past sent many suicide bombers into the cities of Israel. The moral reasoning in the West's position is clear. But along with it I feel there needs to be a full understanding that as long as a force as powerful and as representative as Hamas is entirely excluded there is unlikely to be meaningful progress towards real peace in the wider conflict. And while the West has taken the firmest possible line with Hamas, its pressure on Israel to end its decades of military occupation of the Palestinian Territories is almost negligible.

But my Gaza years were not only about war and politics. The Strip became my home, and between the thousands of stories, the deadlines and the headlines, I came to know its gentler sides rather well. For example, there's nowhere I would rather take breakfast than the terrace of the al-Deira Hotel. Just below you, the Mediterranean washes on to Gaza Beach. And you can watch the fishing boats, their yellow hulls catching the morning sun, emerge from the harbour and begin to dance in the swell. In the evenings, when there's a warm breeze out of the desert, it's a fine thing to eat fish or shrimp and talk with friends somewhere on the waterfront, or at a party on a rooftop. And of course, more than the place, it is the people that you remember. Gazans have weaknesses like everyone else, and God knows their society is as chaotic and anarchic as any that I have come across. But anyone who really knows Gaza will tell you that you often find in people there a largeness of spirit and a remarkable capacity for warmth and friendship – and I certainly experienced that. Gazans are robust, and they tell you what they think, and they probably have to be that way to raise children, make careers and pursue dreams in what is one of the toughest corners of the world.

In my last days in Gaza I saw its darkest side, very close up. I was kidnapped by a group called the Army of Islam. It held me in solitary confinement for nearly four months, during which time I was moved between several hideouts in a neighbourhood on Gaza City's east side. There were moments when I believed that death was a possibility, and I was afraid that I might be held for years. My captivity was far and away the hardest thing that I have ever had to endure – the most appalling experience of my life. Certainly there were times during it when I wished I had never come to Gaza, when I wished that I had never heard of it. But I was lucky. I survived. Given time, I may even feel that I am a little stronger for what I went through. And in retrospect, all things considered, I am very glad that I came to know the Gaza Strip.

THE ISRAELI ARMY COMES CALLING

This visit to the West Bank took place a year before Alan's posting to Gaza. He was making a radio documentary, and staying with a family in the city of Nablus gave him the chance to find out what everyday life was like in a place occupied by Israeli soldiers. (8 March 2003)

THE BEAM FROM THE SEARCHLIGHT caught the house, and the living room around us was suddenly awash with light. We stood motionless, listening to the Israeli armour grind slowly up the street. Would the soldiers pass by, or were they coming for us? They stopped at our gate. It was two in the morning, and it seemed that in a moment the troops would be pounding on our door. We had heard their loudspeaker earlier, ordering people to come out of their homes with their hands on their heads. But then the patrol gunned its engines. It was turning and moving on.

Leila began to laugh softly. 'Now you know why we smoke so much,' she said. I knew all along that even if we were ordered out, my identity card would show that I was a foreign journalist, and I'd be left alone. But for a moment, standing in the beam of the searchlight, you did get a little of the sense of what it is to be a Palestinian when the Israeli army comes calling in the night.

The family that I was staying with are not in any way militant, or even political. But, like all Palestinians, they dread any encounter with the army. A degree of humiliation is always possible. Perhaps there'll be some abuse; an insult, perhaps a slapping for a man who steps out of line. And then there is even the chance of some terrible misunderstanding in the darkness; a nervous young soldier, and a burst of fire.

Back in Jerusalem last summer I remember going through the wreckage of a café where a suicide bomber had struck. A survivor called Nouri Isaacs told me how a chance decision to sit on one side of the café rather than the other had probably saved his life. Nouri went into grotesque detail, telling me how the person he was chatting to had had his ribcage broken by the bomber's head, which had shot across the café like a cannonball.

The Israeli soldiers out in the night, pounding on the doors of Nablus, would tell you that they were on a mission to end those kinds of Palestinian attacks. The army searches for militants from organisations like the al-Aqsa Martyrs' Brigades, which was formed in Nablus. The soldiers would say that if a potential bomber was hiding somewhere in our area, then catching him might save a dozen Israeli lives; and in that case some broken sleep for my friend Khaled and his neighbours would be a small price to pay. But a Palestinian might argue that if Israel was not occupying and expanding its presence on the West Bank then there might not be any suicide bombers.

And so the argument goes on; the occupation continues and, close up, its violence is particularly shocking. During my twelve days in Nablus, the Israelis shot seven people dead, including two ambulance men and a retarded boy. Nablus is a city where anyone so much as disobeying an order to halt during the curfew knows that he is risking the army's deadly fire.

The occupation in its current, especially intense, form seems to crowd into all the corners of the lives of ordinary Palestinians, surfacing in almost every conversation in one way or another. It has smashed the economy and crippled the education system. But in the chaos of what feels like a collapsing society, there is at times a strange degree of normality.

As the Israelis exchanged fire one afternoon with militants in the city centre, just a few streets away people carried on doing business. I watched a young mum glance around the corner of an alleyway to check that it was safe for her kids to cross and perhaps carry on with the shopping. And, despite everything, people in Nablus seemed surprisingly ready to laugh at their strange and violent predicament. You kept coming across a seam of dark humour.

My friend Khaled says that when he was a child he spent a whole intifada throwing stones at Israeli soldiers but he never managed to actually hit one. He says it used to make him wonder if the Israelis really were the chosen people. His stone-throwing wasn't entirely without impact, though. He once hit his brother by mistake. Even the intifada has its friendly fire.

But the moment I'll probably remember longest came after the Israelis had been ransacking Nablus's old quarter, the Casbah, for four days. The city's mayor called for a peaceful protest. At eight-thirty exactly that evening people began, en masse, to let out Islam's famous cry: 'Allahu Akbar' – God is great! Men and women, the young and the old came out on to thousands of balconies and rooftops in driving rain to shout at the top of their voices – over and over again. Their cries and whistles began to merge and swell. In the end, it seemed that the whole city was roaring into the night demanding that God and the world hear its rage and defiance.

In the morning the Israeli army pulled out of the Casbah.

LIFE ON GAZA BEACH

Despite difficult times in the Middle East, where neither Israelis nor Palestinians were moving closer to peace, both Jews and Arabs were trying to enjoy their summer holidays, and how better than with a day out at the seaside? The Gaza Strip does have a beach, but danger is never far away.

(21 August 2004)

IT WAS A HOLIDAY AFTERNOON in high summer. Gaza Beach was a great mass of people. The waves were thick with swimmers. On top of their rickety, wooden tower, the lifeguards were at battle stations. As they struggled to control the masses they blasted on whistles and roared into megaphones: 'You in the boat – get away! Get away from the swimmers. Get away!' Soon it became clear how real the dangers were. Three lifeguards went racing into the waves. They came back up the beach with a thin, unconscious boy in their arms. There were frantic efforts to revive him on the sand below the tower, but his life was slipping away. He was taken to a hospital, but we heard later that he'd died.

The lifeguard in charge of tower number three was Samehh. He's a huge, handsome, easy-going man who watches the waves from behind wrap-around sunglasses. But his flashing smile was gone now. He had done his best to save the boy, but it hadn't been enough. He was saddened as he sat down to talk about his troubles. Friday afternoons like this were the

worst, Samehh said. It's the Muslim day off, and for
the lifeguards it feels like half of Gaza comes to the
beach. And Samehh says that no matter how much the
lifeguards bark and shout, most people just don't
listen. And that's not really a surprise to anyone who
knows this often anarchic society. And there's another
factor: in poverty-stricken Gaza there are no pools
where you can learn to swim. Most people have to
begin in the dangerous currents at the beach.

From a safety point of view, it doesn't help that all the
women go in fully clothed, complete with veils
preserving their Muslim modesty. Then there's the
lack of equipment. You may have seen lifeguarding
being done Los Angeles-style, as in the *Baywatch* TV
series. Well, what goes on at Gaza Beach is rather
different. Samehh and his men don't have *Baywatch*'s
radios, high-powered launches and helicopter. In fact
they don't even have a dinghy. The men of tower
number three are underpaid and madly overworked. Is
there anywhere in the world, I wonder, where it's
tougher to be a lifeguard? But Samehh and his crew *are*
the heroes of Gaza Beach, and they have a fantastic
record. The drowning that I witnessed was actually the
first for years while the guards were on duty. When
they're not there, in the evenings, it's a different story.
Twenty people drowned last summer; but as long as
the lifeguards are on patrol, it's possible to have the

time of your life on Gaza Beach and many, many thousands of Gazans do. Huge Palestinian families, eight-, ten- or even fifteen-strong come down. They pitch camp on the sand and let the kids run wild. They go shrieking and screaming into the surf. High overhead, hundreds of kites dance on the wind. And all the time the beach cafés with their streaming flags and banners and multi-coloured awnings are blasting out Arabic pop music.

The Gaza Strip really is just that, a strip. It is only twenty-five miles long, and in places less than four wide. A third of that is taken up by less than 8,000 Israeli settlers and the soldiers who guard them. Crammed into what remains are well over a million Palestinians. This is one of the most crowded places on earth. In the Jabalia refugee camp they joke that they have the same population density as Manhattan – but without the skyscrapers to go with it. You hear stories of families with eleven children living in two rooms. There's no space left in Gaza; no parks, no grass. But there is the beach. It's Gaza's only playground. As Samehh the lifeguard put it, it's where people go to breathe.

The Israeli occupation and the violence that surrounds it colours every aspect of life here. And with the intensified conflict of the Palestinian uprising has come crushing poverty. In some places up to 60 per cent of men have no work. These are some of the poorest people in the Middle East, but of course, Gaza Beach comes cheap. The youngsters can bounce around in the surf for nothing. You can fly a kite for free. A camel ride only costs a few shekels. And almost anyone can afford the sweet potatoes that are roasted in the blazing, wood-fired ovens that are dragged slowly down the beach on the back of donkey carts.

The Israelis always fear that suicide bombers might emerge from Gaza and strike at their cities. They make it extraordinarily hard for Palestinians to leave the Strip. Army helicopters and pilotless spy planes often circle overhead. Even down on the shore you sometimes see Israeli gunboats cruising in the blue distance. The sense of claustrophobia is intense. This place has been called the world's biggest prison. But, for a few hours at least, the light and the space and the fun to be had on Gaza Beach provide tens of thousands of the people of the Strip with a much-needed Great Escape.

DEATH ON SIKKERT STREET

Another violent week in the Gaza Strip saw Israeli forces battling Palestinian militants around the densely crowded Jabalia refugee camp. A few days earlier, Palestinian suicide bombers had killed sixteen Israelis in the town of Beersheba. Israel responded by killing fourteen Hamas militants in an air attack on Gaza City. Then the Israeli army pushed into the north of the Strip in an attempt to stop Hamas launching rockets at targets in southern Israel. (11 September 2004)

THE JABALIA REFUGEE CAMP is home to 100,000 people. It's a great tangle of alleyways and a jumble of badly made buildings. And this crowded camp has the toughest reputation. It was in the streets of Jabalia that the first Palestinian uprising began. Now it's a stronghold of groups like Hamas and Islamic Jihad, the hard men of this second intifada. When the Israeli army swept up to the gates of Jabalia, with its tanks and bulldozers and snipers, all of Gaza had a sinking feeling. People were going to get killed.

A wide, sandy track called Sikkert Street soon became a deadly place to be. The Israelis took up a position at one end. And every few minutes they sent machine-gun fire up the road. Palestinian fighters were taking cover at the corners. As always, they wore black masks over their faces. They can't allow themselves to be identified by Israeli spotters, or informers within the camp. Some were in camouflage combat gear, but many had just come in jeans and T-shirts. They wore around their heads the green or yellow strips of cloth that displayed their loyalties, to Hamas, or the al-Aqsa

Martyrs' Brigades or Islamic Jihad. And they came with whatever worn-out rifles they had. One carried some battered-looking rocket-propelled grenades on his back. The militants were hopelessly outgunned in their contest with the Israeli tanks and the attack helicopters that circled endlessly overhead. The only advantage that the men in masks had was their knowledge of the alleyways that they grew up in.

They are what the Palestinians call 'the Resistance'. And their confrontation with the Israelis has what can be a deadly attraction for the boys and teenagers of the camp. Large excited crowds of them, some no more than eight or nine years old, gathered around the fighters on Sikkert Street. They peered around the walls at the Israeli tanks. Some would take a few strides out into the road and then scramble for cover when the machine-guns roared. On the other side of Jabalia I watched tiny figures running for their lives across open ground, the bullets throwing up the sand around them. They'd crept closer and closer to the Israelis, who had suddenly opened fire.

It's hard to know quite what goes through the minds of these children – why they take such deadly risks. A while ago, during another Israeli raid, I remember watching a teenager in an orange T-shirt with a slingshot. It was the classic David and Goliath image of the Palestinian uprising. All afternoon he had stood under the sun, and the Israeli guns, whipping his sling round and round before firing stones at two tanks. Several other rock-throwers were shot and wounded next to him in the course of the afternoon. And he told me later that a cousin had died flinging stones at the same crossroads a few months earlier.

Certainly the children are driven by an utter loathing of everything Israeli. They come from families who lost their homes in the war that led to the creation of the Jewish state in 1948. Their grandparents retreated to the grim camps of Gaza – and even there they've had to endure nearly forty years of Israeli occupation. For the youths of Jabalia, any opportunity to confront the enemy is a vast temptation. It's a chance to strike some tiny symbolic blow for Palestine's cause.

But also very much present are more basic impulses, like bravado and the simple, foolish showing-off that you get whenever you have fifty or more teenagers in one place. The stone-throwing is an escape from the despair and the boredom of life in the camps – it promises the thrill of real danger. For their part, the Israelis would certainly say that the youths were being driven on by callous leaders who ought to be restraining them, rather than letting them risk their lives pointlessly. The army says it has to open fire to force back the rock-throwers because they can provide cover for the gunmen. But if I struggle to understand what motivates the boys with the stones, I also wonder quite how the soldier deals with pulling his trigger and watching a nine-year-old slump in the dust.

The Israeli operation is aimed at preventing militants from firing their rockets at targets in neighbouring southern Israel. Groups like Hamas have launched hundreds of such attacks during the past four years of the Palestinian uprising. The rockets are crudely made and rarely cause serious injury or damage. But they have posed enough of a threat to make life miserable and dangerous for people in the Israeli town of Sderot, where two civilians, including a little boy, were killed by missiles during the summer. Hamas stepped up its rocket attacks on Tuesday after the Israelis killed fourteen militants in an air strike. It was this wave of missile fire that had prompted the army's advance on Jabalia.

Near the centre of the camp, under a huge blue tent on some waste ground, I found the friends and family of a man called Mohammad Ezzedine. They were gathering to mourn his death. He was twenty-four years old. He was just recently married, and his wife is pregnant with his first child. By profession, Mohammad was a tailor. He had been trying to get work in the morning, but that had meant crossing that deadly, sandy track – Sikkert Street. He was shot in the chest and killed.

For a moment, Mohammad's brother Rajab emerged from his grief to focus on the madness of the world around him. He argued that Hamas had the right to rocket the Israelis, because the Israelis, he said, were occupying Palestinian land.

As he spoke, Jabalia echoed to the sound of more gunfire on Sikkert Street.

THE KIDNAP CRAZE

With the deterioration of the political and economic situation in Gaza, law and order problems were worsening; disgruntled militia groups and angry clans were kidnapping foreigners. Aid workers and journalists were increasingly concerned.
(14 January 2006)

THE NEWS NEVER REALLY STOPS happening, but it does have its lulls. And in the West at least, in that week between Christmas and New Year, it can almost dry up altogether. But as 2005 drew to a close, events here helped fill the news-less void. An English family had got into big trouble in what, to Europeans, sounds like the last place on earth, the southern end of the Gaza Strip. But like everybody in Gaza, I was always sure that Kate Burton, the young human rights worker who'd been kidnapped, would emerge safe and well along with her parents.

We'd seen all this before. About seventeen foreigners have been kidnapped in the past year. In Iraq an abduction can end in the most brutal murder. But fortunately Gaza isn't Iraq, nothing like it. So far, all the foreigners kidnapped here have been freed quite quickly and unharmed. Often they've been used as bargaining chips, a way for a group of gunmen to get attention.

Gaza is awash with bands of militants, the al-Aqsa Martyrs' Brigades, the Jenin Brigade, the Abu Ali

Mustafa Brigades and so on. They used to attack the occupying Israeli troops and settlers. But the settlements were abandoned in the autumn when the army pulled out, and now the boys from the brigades find themselves with time on their hands. They want proper jobs in this poverty-stricken place and usually they want to be allowed to join the security services. It's ironic really. Gaza is the only place in the world where your kidnapper's one demand is that he should be allowed to become a policeman.

And the kidnap craze has thrown up moments of black humour. The gunmen are not always crack-division militants; more Keystone Kidnappers. While an Italian journalist was being led off to a hideout he had to climb a fence. And when one of his abductors started the climb he absent-mindedly handed the Italian his gun. Surely it's the first thing they teach you at kidnappers' school: never give the hostage your machine-gun.

And the whole business of kidnapping goes very much against the local social grain. Palestinians are extremely hospitable people, and one of the dangers of being abducted here must be that you'll get fed to death.

The other day I heard that a foreign journalist wrongly thought he was about to be snatched and, being

Japanese, he went into martial arts mode. Just part of the madness of Gaza, a Japanese journo mistakenly kung-fu fighting in a refugee camp. I wonder how long he went at it before they could persuade him that it wasn't necessary.

But of course being taken away by armed men is no joke. I dread it, and Palestinian colleagues and the BBC's safety advisors are doing everything they can to help me avoid it. But if my turn does come I will be terrified. The trouble is, the fewer foreigners there are around, the greater the danger, and there are now very, very few foreigners in Gaza.

What you fear most is a bungled rescue attempt. Winkling out a hostage safely isn't easy, even for the world's best-trained police, and Gaza's finest couldn't really be described in that way. And the kidnap game is changing, becoming more political. When the Burton family was freed their kidnappers made a series of demands of the British and Israeli governments.

The gunmen also threatened to kidnap internationals who may come to monitor the parliamentary elections in a few weeks' time. There are suspicions that elements in the ruling establishment fear they'll lose out badly. The latest abductions may have been part of an effort to sabotage the electoral process. Some people, it seems, would rather not have independent foreigner observers around just at the moment. And perhaps that was behind the mysterious bombing of the United Nations' Beach Club. In Gaza's rather austere, Islamic moral climate, it's become almost impossible to buy alcohol. The UN Club was the one exception. It was the only bar on the Strip, and now it's gone. Two bombs took the roof off.

It's true that the Beach Club bar sometimes had a rather forlorn air, just one or two lonely drinkers wondering how they ever came to wash up on Gaza's shore. But there were many good nights too: summer evenings on the terrace overlooking the moonlit harbour and a warm desert breeze out of Sinai rustling the palm trees. With the Beach Club in ruins, Gaza doesn't feel quite the same.

THE MISSING SOLDIER

There was a major escalation in the conflict when militants captured an Israeli soldier close to Gaza's border. Israel carried out nightly air raids and repeatedly sent in tanks and troops. Gazans feared there could be worse to come. (1 July 2006)

YEARS AGO, WHEN AN OLD PALESTINIAN
statesman dropped out of a leadership race a journalist
accused him of being scared of losing. He replied that
he was not scared of losing – he was scared of
winning. What he meant was that anyone who takes
on the challenge of running this place is asking for
trouble.

After nearly forty years of Israeli occupation,
Palestinian society is filled with a sense of having
endured vast injustice. It is mired in despair and badly
divided. There are too many guns, too many armed
factions and not nearly enough hope of something
better to come. The best of governments would
struggle here. And Hamas came to the task with an
attitude towards Israel that guaranteed that it would
quickly be engulfed by problems.

In the past Hamas suicide bombers have hammered at
Israel's cities, taking hundreds of lives. Hamas called
the bombs in the cafés and the buses 'resistance to
occupation'. But the West called it 'terrorism'. It
plunged the new government into economic and

diplomatic isolation. And it will remain an international pariah until Hamas renounces violence and recognises Israel's right to exist. The economic embargo is so severe that civil servants have been paid virtually nothing for nearly four months. Hamas is so desperate that one of its spokesmen was caught trying to smuggle hundreds of thousands of dollars into Gaza in his underclothes. But you cannot run a government like that, and the economy is starting to seize up.

So things were bad enough even before Hamas landed itself in a whole new crisis – the affair of the missing soldier. Hamas militants were among those who raided an army post on Gaza's border on Sunday. In the dawn light they burst out of a tunnel and surprised a slumbering tank crew. The attackers killed two soldiers and led away nineteen-year-old Corporal Gilad Shalit. And when you see pictures of his pale, bespectacled face on television, it is easy to believe that he is as he is described – shy, bright and with a gift for maths. He is every Israeli's 'kid next door'.

And now they are watching him live their nightmare. He is somewhere in the depths of Gaza, in the hands of their most formidable enemy.

Israel holds Hamas entirely responsible for the soldier's fate. It has rejected any talk of freeing any of its several thousand Palestinian prisoners in return for his release. If Corporal Shalit dies, the assassination of Hamas leaders is a real possibility. Already they have largely disappeared from public view. And Israel has put behind bars the movement's political elite in the West Bank. The whole Hamas government project is now in jeopardy. And there is no doubt that the soldier is in great danger. A few days ago the body of another Israeli teenager was found, killed in the West Bank by Palestinian militants.

The crisis surrounding Corporal Shalit has caused huge international concern. The French President, Jacques Chirac, the Pope and the United Nations Secretary General, Kofi Annan, have all appealed for a peaceful outcome. But the Abu Auda family is not counting on that. I sat with them in the cool of their terrace overlooking the farmland around the town of Beit Hanoun. Just beyond the date palms lay the border, and Israel. And the Abu Audas knew that at any time Israeli tanks might come pouring through the maize fields hunting for Corporal Shalit. They have endured numerous incursions, and they knew well what the next one would be like. Helicopter gunships would clatter overhead, there would be gunfire, and the tanks would shake the earth and fill the night with their fumes and the roar of their engines.

It would be terrifying. But as he sat in a long white gown, looking out at the fields, old Abu Shadi Abu Auda said that he was not going anywhere. This was his home, he said, and he would not be leaving.

And Palestinians like him look on at the international attention being focused on the missing soldier with something close to contempt. They see him as a kind of prisoner of war. It is hard to overstate their loathing for the Israeli army. It is the machine that has subjected them to decades of military occupation. Many Palestinian civilians have been killed and their deaths often go largely unnoticed.

A few weeks ago the Israeli air force struck at a leading militant on a busy street in Gaza. The blast caught the Amin family as they passed in their car. A little girl called Mariyah had her spinal cord cut by a bit of shrapnel. She will never move her arms or legs again, she will never even be able to breathe again without the help of a machine, and she is only three years old. Her mother, her grandmother and her brother all died in the Israeli attack. But the Amin family's tragedy went almost unremarked in the wider world – Jacques Chirac, the Pope and Kofi Annan said nothing.

PALESTINIANS KILLING PALESTINIANS

Friction between competing Palestinian factions was increasingly resulting in gun battles and few people in Gaza believed the rival groups were about to settle their differences. (7 October 2006)

GAZA IS BATTERED, poverty-stricken and over-crowded. It's short of money, short of space, short of hope and many other things. But it's not short of guns. There are about a dozen different, official security forces. Alongside the police and the army, there's the Presidential Guard, there's the Preventive Security Unit and so on. There are more security men here per head of population than almost anywhere on earth, but sadly they deliver very little in the way of security. That's partly because there's also a great slew of militias that sprang up to fight nearly forty years of Israeli occupation.

And in addition to the al-Aqsa Martyrs' Brigades and Islamic Jihad and the like there are even more freestyle characters, gunmen who look after the interests of their powerful clans. And all these forces merge and rub along together in the chaos of Gaza.

Of course there are tensions of many kinds. And last Sunday, 'Black Sunday', they exploded. As you drove through the streets that morning you could see trouble coming on every corner. Hamas had flooded Gaza City with its crack division. Powerfully built, bearded and heavily armed men in black. The Hamas-controlled government had ordered them to move against soldiers and policemen, who were on strike and barricading roads in protest at not being paid. Hamas had warned that it was ready, in its words, to 'beat with iron fists'. And by the end of the morning the middle of town was a battleground, a great screaming riot of fleeing civilians and gunmen blazing away at one another.

The Hamas men were clashing with elements in the security forces generally regarded as loyal to the Fatah faction. But in the end it was Palestinians killing Palestinians, and for me the low point came when one set of gunmen took over the roof of Gaza's Centre for Conflict Resolution.

The next day, in a much quieter setting, I met a man called Maher. He knows what it can mean when a powerful armed force decides that it is going to 'beat with iron fists' in the heart of a busy city. He was trying to come to terms with the loss of his fifteen-year-old son, Hussein. The family was mourning in the traditional way, receiving condolences from friends and relatives in the shade of a canopy set up outside their home on Masjid As-Salaam Street. Hussein was walking back from school when he was caught in the gunfight around the Bank of Palestine.

Nobody will ever know whether it was a Hamas or a Fatah bullet that struck him in the head. Maher is a school inspector who specialises in the work of maths departments. He's a man of standards and logic and of course he was appalled by the senselessness of it all. He said he could accept it if his son had died for the Palestinian cause, but not this. 'We live in a jungle,' he said. 'Even if you know who killed someone there is no law to punish him.' And of course Maher is right. Tearing at one another is the last thing that Palestinians should be doing right now. They have way too many problems already.

The Israeli army has been on the offensive here all summer: confronting its militant enemies but also inflicting much suffering on many civilians. Although the West continues to support the moderate President Mahmoud Abbas, it's stopped all funds reaching the Hamas-controlled government because it refuses to renounce violence and accept Israel's right to exist.

It's very much a time for Palestinians to try to stand together, but I'm not so surprised that they can't.

Put yourself in Gaza's position. Imagine for a moment that your society was heavily armed but very poor and crammed into one of the most crowded places on earth. Imagine that about 40 per cent of your people had no job. Imagine that many of those who did work had barely been paid for half a year. Imagine that where you live the borders were usually shut, making it impossible to leave. Imagine that the army of the powerful neighbouring state had killed well over 200 of your people in recent months. Imagine that America was trying to break your newly elected government because it refused to recognise that neighbouring state, which was actually occupying your territory. Imagine, too, that that government of yours was intent on throwing out all past peace agreements with the neighbours and the world and consequently leading you into crushing poverty and isolation.

How would your society cope with pressures like those? Maybe, eventually, there would be some street fighting.

When the American Secretary of State Condoleezza Rice toured the region the other day she acknowledged that there was real hardship in Gaza and she promised to do more to help. But she was also keen to beef up the Presidential Guard, the same force that seized the rooftop of the Conflict Resolution Centre. But what Gaza needs is political solutions. It really doesn't need more guns.

A FAINT SENSE OF HOPE

Moments of peace in Gaza were few and far between. The violent conflict between the militants and the Israeli army seemed relentless. So when a ceasefire was finally agreed it brought, for a time at least, a rare and very welcome spell of calm.

(2 December 2006)

ONE MORNING SOME MONTHS AGO, on the edge of Beit Hanoun, I sat with Abu Shadi Abu Auda looking at the sand dunes that washed up to his terrace. Just beyond a scattering of date palms lay Israel. Many times the army has swept into this corner of Gaza and Abu Shadi's home had recently been hit by shell fire. Half the terrace was a heap of smashed masonry.

We sipped tea and Abu Shadi, a farm labourer in his fifties, reflected on the dangers. He was a dignified figure, very much the respected, grey-haired head of the family. He couldn't move his children to a safer place. He had nowhere else to go. And anyway, he seemed calmly prepared to stick out whatever the army might bring.

Not long after we chatted that summer morning, the storm came and Abu Shadi Abu Auda was killed. His family says he was shot by Israeli troops at his front door. He had dashed out to see what had happened after his son's neighbouring home had been hit by a missile. Abu Shadi's fifteen-year-old daughter,

Hannan, had also raced into the alleyway behind him. She was hit with eight bullets, and died later in hospital.

The Israeli army told me that it only fired at a building from which its soldiers were attacked that night, and that civilians had been caught in the crossfire. Abu Shadi's wife said her family had nothing to do with militant activity. She was just unlucky enough to live on a kind of front line.

Israel said that its five-month assault on Gaza was intended to strike at the many militants here. I've met these men on tense and dangerous days when the army has been hunting them in the alleyways of the refugee camps. Often they are from families that lost homes in what is now Israel in the war of 1948. They believe that Israel sits on their Palestinian land. They are determined to fight it to the end, and they are convinced that in generations to come, and with the help of Allah, Israel will be swept away. Day after day they've fired rockets into Israeli towns and villages. These are crudely made devices and they don't often kill but they are meant to. And it's made no difference to the militants that their rockets have been falling on civilians. In fact, such is their loathing for their enemy that when an Israeli woman in her fifties was killed last month the Hamas and Islamic Jihad organisations fought to claim the credit.

The militants said their rocket fire was retaliation for the army's attacks in what was an uneven contest. Over the past five months five Israelis have been killed. In the same period about 400 Palestinians have died. There have been insane running battles in the fields that pitted stone-throwing Palestinian teenagers and men with rifles against tanks. Every day there were funerals, each of them an explosion of rage and grief. But now, suddenly, it's all stopped. There's a ceasefire, and at last a wonderful calm has settled on Gaza.

On the first day of the truce I was back in battered Beit Hanoun. I found a man called Mohammad Adwan sitting in a plastic chair on Hamad Street. He was chatting to his wife and children and enjoying the unexpected peace. Plastered to the wall above them was a photograph of Mohammad's brother. He was killed on Hamad Street three weeks ago in an Israeli artillery barrage. He had been trying to rescue his neighbours as the shells crashed down. Nearly twenty people were killed altogether in what the army said was a mistaken misdirected attack. All of them were civilians. Mohammad Adwan said simply: 'Our children are scared, and their children are scared. To live in peace is better.'

To almost everyone's dismay, in those first hours the new truce was threatened briefly by another volley of missiles from the Palestinian side. 'That's enough with the rockets,' said Mohammad wearily. 'That's enough.'

But a little further down Hamad Street an old man called Abdelhadi said that there had to be more than a mere silencing of the guns. Sitting beside the barn where he tends chickens, he said that there had to be a just peace. He said that there needed to be an end to the Israeli occupation of all Palestinian land, that eventually there had to be a Palestinian state that would live alongside Israel. Both nations, the old man said, should have their rights.

People here know the rhythms of the politics of the Middle East all too well. They don't really believe that the calm will last. But right now there is something very unusual in the air in Gaza – there is the faintest sense of hope.

KIDNAPPED

Alan was nearing the end of his BBC posting in Gaza
when he was kidnapped in March 2007. He was
eventually released after 114 days in captivity.
(25 October 2007)

THE KIDNAPPERS HAD FORCED ME to lie face down on the floor. But after they left, and the small, bare room had fallen silent, I rolled over and pulled myself slowly into a sitting position. My wrists were handcuffed behind my back, and a black hood had been pulled down over my head. And as I sat there, in danger and afraid, I had a great sense of being at the very lowest point of my life.

It had begun out in the spring sunshine, on the streets of Gaza City. A saloon car had suddenly surged past mine, and then pulled up – forcing me to stop. A young man emerged from the passenger side and pointed a pistol at me. I had reported many times on the kidnapping of foreigners in Gaza. Now, as I always feared it might, my turn had come. The figure with the pistol and another gunman forced me into their car, and as we sped off I was made to lie on the back seat. A hood had been shoved over my face, but through it I could see the sun flickering between the tower blocks. I could tell that we were heading south and east, towards the city's rougher neighbourhoods.

Most kidnappings in Gaza were carried out by disgruntled militant groups seeking the attention of the authorities in some minor dispute. And always the Westerner was freed within a week or so, shaken but unharmed.

But the game had changed last summer. A much more sinister group had emerged and seized two members of a team from the American Fox News network. They were freed, but only after being forced to make videotaped denunciations of the West and a public conversion to Islam.

Of course this was serious. In the claustrophobic, intense, violent sliver of land that is Gaza, there was now a shadowy organisation that thought in terms of waging jihad on the West. I knew it was likely to strike again, targeting the few dozen members of Gaza's foreign community. And so, with the help of the BBC's security experts, I did everything I could to reduce the risk of capture. I moved to a better-protected apartment. I filmed less in the streets, switched cars and made sure that my movements in the city were always random and unpredictable.

And set against the danger, I felt that Gaza's story was important. It is at the centre of the Palestinian drama which in turn lies at the heart of the rising tensions between the East and the West that have become the defining story of our time.

So, in consultation with senior colleagues, I decided that the risks were worth taking and I stayed in Gaza. And I did manage to keep out of the grasp of the kidnappers almost to the end. When the man with the pistol emerged from the white saloon, I had just sixteen days left until I was due to leave for good.

As I lay on a thin mattress on the floor, late on the first night of my captivity, the door opened. Its frame was filled by a tall figure in a long white robe. He stood for a moment looking down at me, swathed in a red chequered headdress that completely masked his face. The jihadi leader had arrived. He stepped into the room and sat down heavily on a white plastic chair. 'Alan Johnston, we know everything,' he said in English.

He said that my kidnapping was about securing the release of Muslims jailed in Britain. Later, my captors, the Army of Islam, would describe me as a prisoner in what they see as the war between Muslims and non-Muslims. When I started to say that Britain wouldn't negotiate, the man in the chair cut me off. He said that the British would be forced to listen.

But mostly the voice emerging from the mask was calm and even kindly. He said that I wouldn't be killed, that I would be treated well, in keeping with Islamic codes of conduct towards prisoners. Crucially, he said that I would eventually be allowed to leave. I asked when, but he just said: 'When the time is right.'

Did he mean weeks, or months, or longer? It was impossible to say. But I was left with a disturbing sense that what was about to happen would be protracted and life-changing. When it was over, he said, I would write a book about my experience and even that I would finally get married.

But how far could I trust the masked man? Did his word really count for anything – couldn't he simply change his mind? And I wondered if he really was a leader of the group. Perhaps, in reality, others would decide my fate.

I did fall asleep again, but I was woken by two men coming into the room. They handcuffed me and put the black hood back over my head and led me slowly out into the cold of the night. There was no word of explanation, and as my mind searched for one in that terrifying moment of uncertainty, I feared, as I walked into the darkness, that I might be going to my death, that I was being taken somewhere to be shot. But the tension eased as I began to realise that the men were only moving me to another building and what would, for a time, become my cell.

In that room, on the roof of an apartment block, all I had was a narrow, sagging bed and two plastic chairs. There was no television, or radio, or book, or pen, or paper. I'd been stripped of my watch; I could only tell the time by the passage of the sun and the five calls to prayer from nearby mosques. I had had to throw away my disposable contact lenses on the first day, and my eyes are weak. And so, in this blurred, empty room I began to try to come to terms with the disaster that had engulfed me.

I paced backwards and forwards across the cell. Five strides, then a turn, and five strides back. Mile, after mile, after mile. Imagine yourself in that room. Imagine pacing, or just sitting for three hours. For five hours. For ten hours. After you had done twelve hours, you'd still have four or five more before you could hope to fall asleep. And you would know that the next day would be the same, and the next, and the one after that, and so on, and on, and on.

As one empty day slid slowly into another, the seriousness of my situation became more and more apparent. It's hard to strike at Britain from Gaza. There's no British business there, and the British Council library was burnt down last year by an angry mob. Almost all that Britain had left in Gaza was the BBC. And in the BBC there was only one British citizen: me. And the jihadis had me, like a bird in a cage. Britain never does deals with kidnappers so why, I couldn't help worrying, would I ever be freed? I thought of the Western hostages who had been held for years in Beirut in the eighties, and I wondered if their fate might now be mine.

The first crisis came in the form of a bout of illness. The food was quite reasonable, Palestinian-style rice or beans or vegetable dishes apparently cooked in a flat just below my room. But my European stomach couldn't cope either with what I was eating or the dirty water. Soon I could feel a swelling just below my ribs and there were many trips to the small, foul-smelling toilet attached to my room, where the floor was always awash with water. I was frightened that I would just get sicker and sicker and I decided I must try to get some control over my diet. In the first weeks I had occasionally been given potato chips and I knew that even the toughest Gazan bacteria couldn't survive the sizzling oil that they were fried in. So I asked just for a plate of chips each day and for my water to be boiled. And those simple elements, along with bread, tomatoes, some fruit and later eggs became the basis of my rather dull, but safer, two meals a day. There was, though, never quite enough food, and I eventually lost ten kilograms. And always I worried, especially when I had a serious allergic reaction later on, that I might fall dangerously ill. I was sure that, if it came to it, the Army of Islam would just let me fade away slowly rather than call off the kidnap because I was sick.

In those first, terrible days, the hardest that I have ever known, I worried very much about the impact my abduction would have on my elderly parents and my sister at home in Scotland. And of course, with that wonderful clarity of hindsight, I deeply, deeply regretted having stayed in Gaza so long and having taken the risks that I had.

One of my lowest moments came during a power cut. I lay in a dwindling pool of candlelight, listening to the shouting, rowing neighbours and occasional gunshots that are all part of the noisy clamour of Gaza's poorer neighbourhoods. I felt very, very far from home, trapped and aghast at how dire my situation was.

Things were, however, just about to get a little better. Desperate for some distraction to ease the psychological pressure, I had repeatedly asked for a radio and amazingly, on the night of that power cut, a guard brought one into my room. Suddenly I had a link with the outside world – a voice in my cell, and something to listen to other than my own frightening thoughts. And through the radio I became aware of the extraordinary, worldwide campaign that the BBC was mobilising on my behalf. It was an enormous psychological boost. And, most movingly, I realised that the vast majority of Palestinians were condemning the kidnappers. Many people in Gaza seemed to appreciate that I had chosen to live among them for years in order to tell their story to the world.

But the radio also brought dreadful news. In those calm, measured tones of the BBC, I heard reports of a claim that I had been executed. It was a shocking moment. I had been declared dead – and I thought how appalling it was that my family should have to endure that. But of course, I knew that I was far from dead, and after a few minutes I couldn't help recalling the famous Mark Twain line about how the reports of his death had been exaggerated.

I was worried, though, that perhaps the announcement of my execution was just a little premature. I knew that my kidnappers' demands were not being met, and I thought that perhaps they had decided to kill me. I felt that I needed to prepare myself for that possibility in the hours ahead. I was sure that if I was to be put to death, the act would be videotaped in the style of jihadi executions in Iraq. If that was to be the last image my family and the world was to have of me, if at all possible I didn't want it to be one of a weeping, pleading, broken man. So through that long night, I lay listening to every sound that might signal the coming of my assassins and tried to gather the strength that I would need if the worst were to happen. But at last the silence was broken by the dawn call to prayer. The night was over. Somehow I felt the danger had passed, and I fell asleep.

But that wasn't the last time that death seemed a possibility. A few weeks later my guard barged into my room with a set of manacles. My wrists and ankles were chained together. And the guard shut my window and put off the light, leaving me in the dark to swelter in Gaza's summer heat. He told me that it was being decided whether I should be put to death in the days ahead. If that was to happen, he said, my throat would be cut with a knife. I didn't quite believe the threat but again, I had to prepare myself for the worst. I'm sure that different people approach something like that in different ways. But I chose to rehearse in my mind exactly what might happen, hoping that somehow that would make the lead-up to any execution a little less shocking, a little less terrifying, and hoping that that might make it easier to preserve some kind of dignity in my final moments. But mercifully, the crisis passed. In fact, the chains came off after just twenty-four hours and as the days went by, the threat of execution seemed to recede again.

Through all this I gradually came to know my guards. One of them, a man in his mid-twenties called Khamees, with a dark, quite handsome face, would be with me almost every day, right through to the kidnap's frightening climax. Like many young men who I had met in Gaza, Khamees was the son of a family that had either fled or been driven from their home in what is now Israel. He had been raised in the poverty of one of Gaza's intensely crowded cities and been drawn to the militant groups that had fought the occupying Israeli army. Khamees had matured into a battle-hardened urban guerrilla. He walked with a limp and had a slightly misshapen torso, the legacy of a wound inflicted by the Israelis. But they weren't his only enemy. He had trouble too with both of Gaza's main factions: Hamas and Fatah. He was a wanted man and he almost never left the succession of flats that were my prisons. He lived confined to the shadows – almost literally in the second of our hideouts, where the shutters on the windows were kept closed and I didn't see the sun or the sky for nearly three months.

Khamees would exercise by pacing up and down the gloomy corridor, counting the laps on his prayer beads. He spent countless hours flipping through the Arabic satellite television channels, and often, far into the night, he would sit in a pale blue robe, reading aloud from the Koran. Occasionally he would let me go through to his room and watch television for an hour or two. And one day he allowed me to see my parents make a televised appeal for my release. After worrying about them so much it was a vast relief to see my father make a powerful and dignified address. And although my mother didn't speak, when I looked into her eyes I was somehow sure that she too had the strength to cope. I felt very bad at having brought the worst of the world's troubles crashing through my parents' peaceful lives, far away on the west coast of Scotland. My kidnappers, the most frightening kind of people, were putting them under appalling pressure and all of Britain was watching. But my parents weren't being broken. They were, in Dad's words, 'hanging in there,' and for me it was their finest hour.

To let me see my parents on television was an act of kindness on the part of my guard and there were certainly others. In the second of our four hideouts, where I was held longest, Khamees allowed the regime to become quite lax. My door was left unlocked so that I could go to a bathroom and even use a kitchen next to my room, where eventually I was boiling water and fixing very simple meals for myself twice a day. And there were moments when Khamees would be friendly, when we would talk a little about Gaza, and about politics or Islam. But mostly I will remember Khamees as a dark and moody figure. Often, for days at a time, he barely spoke to me, refusing to respond if I said hello. Handing me my food, he would just glare at me hard, saying nothing, and a number of times tiny things sent him into frightening rages that I came to dread. It was often easy to imagine that he saw me as a great burden and that he loathed me. And when he smashed me in the face in the final moments of the kidnap I felt that, with Khamees, perhaps all along violence had never been far below the surface.

As the weeks drifted by, and I paced through my wasteland of time, my thoughts often ranged back across my life. I filled many empty hours reflecting on periods in my childhood and phases of my career. I tried to work out the roots of certain aspects of my character and I thought hard again about why one or two important relationships in my past had worked but then eventually lost their way. But much of my mental energy went into the huge effort to confront my many anxieties: the struggle, as I saw it, to keep my mind in the right place. I felt very strongly that in the kidnapping I was facing the greatest challenge of my life and I knew that I would perhaps always measure myself by the way I met it, or failed to meet it. I told

myself that in my captivity there was only one thing
that I might be able to control, my state of mind. And I
struggled to persuade myself that bouts of depression
did nothing to change the hard realities of my
situation, they only weakened me. I tried to strangle
damaging, negative thoughts almost as they emerged,
before they could take hold and drive me down. And
positive thoughts had to be encouraged. Of course, at
first glance, there wasn't much to take heart from in
my situation.

But the fact was that I hadn't been killed and I wasn't
being beaten around. I was being fed reasonably and I
decided that my conditions could have been much,
much worse. Whatever else it was, my Gazan
incarceration wasn't what some Iraqi prisoners had
been forced to endure at Abu Ghraib jail. It wasn't the
Russian Gulag and it certainly wasn't the Nazi death
camps. I felt that I wouldn't be able to pick up a book
again about the Holocaust without feeling a sense of
shame if I were somehow to break down mentally
under the very, very, very much easier circumstances of
my captivity. I thought too that, unfortunately, every
day around the world, people are being told that they
have cancer and that they only have a year or two to
live. But the vast majority of them find the strength to
face the end of their lives with dignity and courage. I,
on the other hand, was just waiting for my life to begin

again, and I told myself that it would be shameful if I couldn't conduct myself with some grace in the face of my much lesser challenge.

And in its search for inspiration, my mind took me down what may sound to you like some rather strange paths. But for me, as impressive as any story of endurance is that of the explorer Ernest Shackleton. After his ship was crushed by the Antarctic ice nearly a century ago, he took a tiny lifeboat and set out across the great wastes of the stormy Southern Ocean. He aimed for an almost unimaginably small island far beyond his horizon and eventually he reached it. And in my prison, I felt that I needed some kind of mental lifeboat to help me cross the great ocean of time that lay before me, aiming for that almost unimaginable moment far beyond my horizon when I might go free. And so I took all the positive thoughts I could muster and lashed them together in my mind, like planks in a psychological raft that I hoped would buoy me up. And in some ways it did. It was one of several mental devices or tricks or props that helped me get through.

In this way, I fought what was the psychological battle of my life. God knows it was hard. And lonely. And there were many dark passages when I edged close to despair. But I was always in the fight, and there was no collapse.

Eventually Gaza's violent politics suddenly shifted against my kidnappers. The powerful Hamas and Fatah factions began a fight to the death. Hour after hour I lay listening to machine-gun and rocket fire in the streets around the apartment block where I was being held. Bad enough, I felt, to be kidnapped, but worse still to be lost in a place that had descended into all-out war. Eventually, though, Hamas managed to seize complete control. It immediately set about imposing what it would regard as order in Gaza and it made ending my high-profile kidnapping a priority.

For the first time my captors seemed shaken and uncertain, but they had a plan. Khamees came in with a plain black briefcase, of a kind that you might see any accountant carry on the London Underground. But he opened it to reveal a suicide bomber's vest, with panels of explosives that closed tight around my stomach as I pulled it on. In a letter the leader, the masked man from the first night, said that I needed to be afraid. He said that Hamas was planning an assault that would turn the hideout into what he called 'a death zone'. The message I had to give via a video camera, dressed in my deadly contraption, was that if there was an attack, I too would die.

But still Hamas was closing in and the Army of Islam prepared for a showdown. A machine-gun nest was set up just under the room where I was being held. And I could hear the group's fighters scramble to their battle stations below me during an exchange of fire as Hamas forces probed their defences. I knew that if Hamas stormed the apartment block they would come all guns blazing and I might well die in the assault. And even if Hamas didn't kill me accidentally, then there was a danger that the kidnappers, furious and frightened, and about to die themselves, might shoot me to prevent my being rescued alive.

Then suddenly one night I was taken downstairs. A hood was put over my head and I was led stumbling out into the darkness as members of the gang began to hit me and slam me against walls and the side of a car, before I was shoved into its back seat.

The kidnappers and the powerful clan that was protecting them seemed to have buckled under Hamas pressure. They had agreed to deliver me up in return for their survival. But I didn't know that as the car began to move slowly towards the Hamas lines and the most terrifying ride of my life began. My guards, with their Kalashnikov rifles on either side of me, were screaming angry; furious no doubt at the failure of the kidnap and scared perhaps that Hamas would kill them anyway, whatever the deal. Khamees struck at my face, and I could taste blood in my mouth. At one of the checkpoints, through the wool of my mask, I could see the muzzle of a rifle inches from my eye and I knew that the guard on my right was roaring that he would put a bullet in my brain if the Hamas men didn't back off. In the extraordinary tension and the confusion it seemed that a gun battle might erupt at any moment and the car would be filled with bullets.

Eventually though, we came to a halt and Khamees dragged me out into the road. I looked up to see an alleyway filled with armed men standing in the street light. Two of them stepped forward and led me away. I was afraid that this was some new gang to which I had now been passed on. But actually these were Hamas men and as we turned a corner, there, standing in a garden, was my old friend and colleague, Fayed Abu Shamalla of the BBC Arabic service. And only then did I know that my kidnap was over and that I was free.

Days later I was back in Scotland, taking that road that I know so well, heading at last for the hills of Argyll and my family. And there, in our house by the sea, in that beautiful, peaceful place, all that happened to me in Gaza began to slide into the past. But the experience of incarceration does have a way of lingering, of haunting the nights. I dream sometimes that I'm in captivity again and I cannot tell you how good it is to wake and gradually realise that, actually, I'm free, safe,

Alan Johnston pictured moments after his release (Reuters)

Alan is escorted to safety by Hamas gunmen (Abid Katib/Getty Images)

back at home, on the shores of Loch Goil. But the nightmares come less frequently now. And although psychologists might say that these are still quite early days, I very much believe that I'm going to be fine.

And the kidnap's legacy is not all bad. With its locks and chains, its solitary confinement and moments of terror, it was a kind of dark education. I lived through things which before I would have struggled to imagine and maybe, in the end, I'll be stronger for that. I've gained too a deeper sense of the value of freedom. Perhaps only if you've ever been some kind of prisoner can you truly understand its worth. Even now, more than three months after I was freed, it can still seem faintly magical to do the simplest things, like walk down a street in the sunshine, or sit in a café with a newspaper. And in my captivity in Gaza, I learnt again that oldest of lessons: that in life, all that really, really matters are the people you love.

ALAN JOHNSTON INTERVIEWED BY TONY GRANT

A few months after his release from captivity, Alan took part in a question-and-answer session with Tony Grant from BBC Radio's *From Our Own Correspondent*.

Q: Why do you think your guards let you have a radio, and just how important was that development?

From the start I knew how psychologically crushing the isolation of my incarceration would be, and in the first hours I asked the masked leader if I could have a radio. And I kept asking my guards for one every chance I got. I told them I needed more human contact. Perhaps they were sorry for me, or perhaps they just wanted me to stop pestering them, but on the seventeenth day one of them walked in with a set. It was a hugely important moment. From then on I wasn't quite so alone. I had been hoping that perhaps the BBC would mount a little local campaign on my behalf to try to keep people in Gaza on my side. But as I listened to the radio, I realised that my colleagues were mobilising support all around the globe. In a display of solidarity, its rivals, such as CNN, Sky and Al Jazeera, were joining the effort, along with countless other smaller journalistic organisations and human rights activists. It was an extraordinary thing to be at the centre of all that, and I found it very moving. I was lost. Buried alive and in the worst trouble that I could imagine, but it felt like the whole world of journalism was saying that I would not be forgotten. To anyone who took part in the campaign in any way, I am grateful. And I got a very strong sense that Britain, especially, was watching. During an interview on the World Service about something else altogether, I heard a woman suddenly say that her eight-year-old son was following my story and that he'd become slightly obsessed with whether I lived or died. A few days later I heard the prime minister, Tony Blair, express his concern for me in Parliament, to a rumble of approval from the House of Commons. And I realised that along with that eight-year-old boy and the prime minister, there were perhaps a few other people here who were also interested in my plight.

Q: *What were the most important messages you received via the radio?*

The BBC broadcast a message on my birthday from my parents, and nothing could have been more important than hearing their voices. But the words of other people who had endured captivity also gave me a tremendous psychological lift. I'll never forget the advice I got from the former Beirut hostage Terry Waite. He said that the mind and the body were extraordinary things, and that I would find more

Staff and colleagues at the headquarters of the BBC World Service, Bush House, London, staging a demonstration calling for Alan to be freed (Peter Macdiarmid/Getty Images)

strength than I might think I had. The words of another ex-Beirut captive, Brian Keenan, also echoed through my mind again and again. He very much knew what to say to someone in my position. He told me that hundreds of thousands of people around the world were lighting a candle for me. 'And we shall not walk away,' he said. It was a simple line, but it seemed to be exactly what I wanted to hear. As I paced up and down my cell I often used to repeat those words in my head: 'And we shall not walk away, and we shall not walk away.' One more ex-hostage, the journalist and author Charles Glass, who was also held in Lebanon, sent an important message, too. At one point during it he said simply, slowly and clearly: 'You will get out,' and then again: 'You will get out.' Of course, he couldn't know that. But he delivered the line in his warm American accent with such conviction that somehow it was easy to believe.

And of course I was moved when old friends sent messages. One reminded me of happier days we had known together in Gaza, and then invited me to Berlin. And soon after I was freed I did go to Berlin, taking up the offer that I'd received in my cell. But sometimes the words that came from complete strangers were as touching as any. A guy in the north of England said: 'I don't know what's going on, mate. But I hope you get back to Blighty soon, and that you can be a bit strong in the meantime.' It just seemed tough, and direct, and friendly, and typically British, and it stuck in my mind.

Q: Some people would argue that too much was made of your case, that you received more publicity than you deserved.

I would agree, and I felt that during my captivity. I used to think that in Colombia, Iraq, the Philippines and elsewhere, there would be other kidnap victims and people unjustly imprisoned who were getting none of the kind of support that I was receiving. I felt that I was – if there is such a thing – the world's luckiest kidnap victim. And when I emerged from captivity I found out that over those first six months of the year

Support for the campaign to set Alan free came from across the
Palestinian territories (Said Khatib/AFP/Getty Images)

Local journalists in Gaza City (above and below Mohammed Abed/
AFP/Getty Images)

Statue to the
Unknown
Soldier in
Gaza City

some forty journalists had been abducted, and that only eight of us had been freed. While I was still back in my cell I decided that if I could, I would use my heightened profile to focus some attention on the forgotten others. And I am now making some effort to do that through work with Amnesty International. But I also want to defend the campaign mounted on my behalf. Dangerous men were repeatedly threatening to slaughter me, and my friends and colleagues at the BBC had very limited options. The British government would never free a prisoner in return for my release, as my kidnappers were demanding, and the BBC could never pay a ransom. To do so might endanger other correspondents. But one thing the BBC could do was generate some attention for my cause, and it did that brilliantly. The campaign gathered momentum and went far beyond the Corporation. From the very top of the BBC, down to its listeners and viewers and readers around the world, this whole remarkable organisation did everything it could for me – and for that, I will be grateful all of my days.

Q: Military people talk about the 'shock of capture', a period of mental turmoil in the initial phase of imprisonment that can give way to a more stable state. Is that what you went through?

It was very much that way. When I began to think that I might be held for years it was as if the ground was opening up beneath me. The anxiety was so intense it was an almost physical sensation. I remember once crouching to pick something up from the floor, but then just staying down there and being filled by a conviction that my life was utterly ruined. It was as if I was being forced to live some waking nightmare, as if what was going on should only really be experienced by other people in films or books – it was hard to believe that this was actually happening to me. But it wasn't like that all the time. There were also much more upbeat spells in those early days, when I would try to believe that it might still all end quite quickly in a deal of some kind. At that stage I hadn't worked out the strategies that I used later to try to control my moods, and I felt that my mind was being rather buffeted around. But I do remember washing up on to firmer mental ground on about the eleventh night. I remember sitting in the plastic chair in my room and being able to contemplate in quite a calm, almost philosophical way what it would mean if I was to be held for years, and just what that would take to endure. Of course that mood eventually evaporated too. But it had shown me that it was possible to reflect on the worst with a degree of composure, and I was always working to try to regenerate that frame of mind.

Sometimes it was quite easy to do that, and sometimes it was hard or even impossible for a while. I would be lost in darker thoughts. But I knew that they needed to be fought, and I was almost always trying to find the strength to do that. That was important not only in terms of my mental health. I had difficult decisions to make, like whether to try to escape, and how best to attempt to work the relationship with the guards. They were matters that I needed to be calm and rational about, if I could. To fall apart mentally might have been dangerous in different ways.

Q: You mention there strategies you used to try to control your mood. Tell us more about that.

In the second hideout there was a window in my room. On the left side, in my mind's eye – in my imagination – I used to write on the wall the sort of damaging, negative thoughts that would swirl through my head: worries about my parents, regrets at having stayed in Gaza, and other fears and anxieties. And on the right side of the window I used to stack up the reasons to be positive, such as they were. I hadn't been killed, I wasn't being beaten, I wasn't chained up, a deal might be done and so on. And the effort then was to almost physically drag my mind on to the right side of the window, to draw it to the right side of the mental equation and fill it with those positive thoughts. I used to tell myself, as I paced up and down the room, that my guards weren't torturing me, but that I might torture myself if I didn't manage to control my mind. I told myself that I could dwell on the negative and make my incarceration even harder, or do everything I could to try to focus on the positive and make it easier.

As I said on the radio, locked in that kind of psychological battle, and desperate for ideas and images that might help get me through, my mind took me down avenues that might sound strange to anyone else. But I quite often used to imagine myself drifting down what I called the River of Time. I used to tell myself that with every passing second it was carrying me towards that almost unimaginable moment when my captivity would somehow end. I used to see myself as a boatman guiding a raft down the great river. And I always looked to steer away from the rougher waters, which symbolised negative thoughts. I tried to head my mental raft towards the calmer stretches of the stream, where my helmsman's mind could be filled with positive notions. I told myself too that the river flowed faster and that time passed quicker in those smoother reaches, and that I must try to stick to them. And I attempted to persuade myself not to focus on the horizon, the symbolic end of the voyage – freedom. I tried to believe that that would come in its own good time. Sometimes I was quite hard on myself. I used to say that if I were to break down, all of my life I would know that when big questions were asked of me in Gaza I had not come up with any good answers. I used to travel with an American journalist in Central Asia who said once: 'All you can expect of yourself in life is one or two substantial moments.' For some reason, the phrase stayed with me. What I took it to mean was that once or twice, when you really need it, you might find more strength in yourself than you would normally expect. And I often told myself that my kidnapping was one of those crises in life that demanded a 'substantial moment' in response, and that I must try to come up with it.

But it is important to say that all those strategies didn't work all the time, by any means. Many days began in what I used to think of as a blue mood. I would gradually have to get the rational side of my brain to engage with those bleak emotions that had taken hold, and try to wear them down.

Q: You talked of drawing strength from the story of the explorer Ernest Shackleton. Were there other sources of inspiration?

Not long before I was captured a friend told me how her father had survived Auschwitz and later married a German woman. He seemed to me to have demonstrated all the best qualities in the human spirit: our capacity to endure, to forgive and to love. And as I have said before, my brief captivity was absolutely nothing – nothing – in comparison to what my friend's father went through. It was not much either set alongside some of the stories that emerged from my radio. There was excellent reporting on the BBC at the time from eastern Congo, where millions have died in recent years almost unnoticed by the wider world. There was one particularly appalling account given by a woman who had been raped numerous times and then forced to kill her own child. Her story helped me set my very much lesser suffering in context.

Q: Did you think much about God while you were locked up? Did you pray?

As moving as anything in all this has been the number of people of all faiths who have told me that they prayed for me. Of course it's impossible to know what influence that may or may not have had in the way things unfolded for me. We live surrounded by much that is mysterious and unknowable. I do think, though, that when anyone demonstrates concern for the suffering of a stranger they are acting in the best traditions of all the great religions. But as for me, I have to say that I was not praying before I was captured, and I didn't feel that it would be right to start because I suddenly found myself in trouble. I think that you have to hope that you have treated other people properly, and tried to live fairly decently, before a crisis erupts. If you have, then maybe you can hope that a God of mercy and love might come to your assistance. But in the course of my work, I have seen a great deal of suffering endured by people who were entirely innocent. And to be honest, that has left me struggling to believe that God does closely manage our individual lives.

Q: *In your lowest moments were you ever suicidal?*

No. The will to live was overwhelming. I desperately wanted to survive and get home – and most of all, back to my family. But I did have a great, no doubt exaggerated, fear of falling seriously ill, and I used to think that if I was dying in unbearable agony with, say, a burst appendix, I would want the option of trying to take my own life. And I did work out how I might do that. In the first hideout there were panes of glass in a small, louvred window in the bathroom, and I thought I might be able to break one and use it to cut my wrists. In the second hideout I had access to knives in the kitchen. And when I was forced to wrestle with the horror of the possibility of execution, I thought that the one thing that could be said for it was that once it was done my suffering would end. In an interview I heard on the radio while I was being held, a woman talked of having endured appalling conditions in a jail in Iran, and she said that when she thought she was about to be shot it was almost a relief. I can now quite easily imagine how, in conditions of captivity much more severe than mine, death might be seen as a bleak but welcome release.

Q: You told us that the security regime in the second hideout wasn't so tight. Did you think of escaping?

At times I was obsessed by thoughts of escape. There were one or two faint possibilities, and I used to give myself a hard time for not trying. I suspected that subconsciously at least I just wasn't brave enough to make an attempt. But every time I thought it through I decided that it would be a mistake. I am not at all a violent person, and I was up against a guard who was a seasoned urban guerrilla. I felt sure that if any escape attempt involved violence I would almost certainly lose. And in the second hideout where the chances were better, even if I had somehow managed to overpower the guard, I didn't know where he kept the crucially important key to the front door. However, an even bigger problem was that I was being held in a neighbourhood that was the stronghold of a clan that was working with my captors. Westerners just didn't go walking the streets in that part of town. I was sure that even if I managed to get out of the flat I would be spotted and picked up again in the alleyways. And so I had to think hard about the consequences of a failed escape attempt. There would surely have been the danger of a beating. I would probably have found myself back in my cell, only now with a couple of broken ribs or a fractured jaw – and that might easily have amounted to a death sentence in a situation where medical assistance would be unlikely to ever come. And no doubt my treatment would have been very much harsher after a failed bid for freedom. I might have been chained up, as I was anyway for one brief period – and remember that I was bracing myself for a period of captivity that I feared might go on for years.

Q: What do you think of the role that Hamas played in your release?

There are some people who claim that Hamas orchestrated my kidnapping as a kind of vast publicity stunt. But I don't believe that. Perhaps what separates me from the conspiracy theorists is that I was on the inside, and able to watch the kidnappers close up as they reacted to the mounting Hamas pressure. One of Gaza's most notorious clans, the Doghmush, was central to my abduction. It protected, led and hosted in its neighbourhood, the jihadist group, the Army of Islam, which actually held me. The Doghmush had certainly been allied with Hamas in the past, but at the time of my kidnapping the clan and the faction were locked in the most bitter blood feud that I had seen in all my time in Gaza. Hamas men had killed several Doghmush in cold blood at a checkpoint just before Christmas. In response the Doghmush were demanding the deaths of a number of Hamas members.

Given that background there was bound to be extreme tension between the clan and the faction once Hamas had dispensed with its rival, Fatah, and taken complete control of Gaza in late June. For many reasons Hamas needed to show quickly that it could deliver what it would regard as law and order. It had to show that it really was in charge. My kidnapping was a kind of test, and if Hamas couldn't solve it, it would have sent a bad signal. The message to other clans or militias would have been that if you are tough enough you can run your own little corner of Gaza and do what you like – that Hamas can tolerate no-go areas. And in the immediate aftermath of the Hamas takeover, in the hideout, I saw signs of real concern among the kidnappers. There was an angry, rather panicky letter to me from the leader of the gang.

The group was clearly worried that Hamas knew where I was being held and planned to storm the apartment. That was when I had to make a video dressed in a suicide bomber's vest and say that if the building was attacked I would be blown up. Soon afterwards I was moved to what the group felt was a more secure apartment block, and as I said on the radio, there were clear preparations for a showdown.

My guard told me that his brother had been arrested and flung in jail by Hamas as it sought to gain leverage and bargaining chips. Later the same man was clearly shocked by a major Hamas sweep that had led to the capture of more people associated with the group – including the brother of one of the leaders. In addition we believe that the most senior figure in the Doghmush clan linked to the kidnap was wounded in a firefight with Hamas men during the abduction. There are many people who would argue that the Hamas takeover of Gaza was damaging in a variety of ways. But in terms of my kidnapping, I think that transformation of the political scene was the key factor in creating the conditions in which I could be freed.

Q: Has your captivity altered the way you think about the people of Gaza?

I had lived in Gaza for years before my kidnap and I was very familiar with its traditions of hospitality and kindness to strangers. In all the turmoil I had witnessed there, before I was kidnapped, I had never been personally threatened. I knew that the behaviour of my captors was an aberration. I also felt that the response of many Palestinians to my plight was remarkable. Demonstrators calling for my release took to the streets repeatedly in the West Bank and Gaza. It was clear that the vast majority of Palestinians bitterly condemned what the Army of Islam was doing.

Most striking of all was the response of the local journalists who had been my colleagues and friends for years. They led the campaign on my behalf with great passion. Five weeks into the drama they even fought with police as they attempted to storm Parliament and demand that the authorities do more to secure my release.

Q: *How do you feel about your captors now?*

So much of my mental effort in captivity was given over to trying to keep control of my mind. I felt that if I let myself hate my captors it could be damaging. Hatred is, of course, such a powerful emotion. Unleashing it, and letting it rage and get a grip, wouldn't have been a good idea. It might have made it harder to stay calm and maintain some control. And I never really did engage with the kidnappers emotionally in any way, apart from being scared of them on occasions. I tried to see them only as a problem, people who I needed to attempt to figure out as coldly and rationally as I could. And now that I am free I still have no real feelings about them.

Q: And what do you think of their political aims? They talked of you being a prisoner in the war between Muslims and non-Muslims.

When you look across the Middle East you see dictatorial regimes, corruption, instability and war. There has been a failure to build really impressive institutions and political systems. And all this is going on in the age of oil – a time when parts of the region have been blessed with fantastic wealth. Arabs might have hoped that that abundance would be used to start regenerating their civilisation, and perhaps restore some of its past glories. I very much believe that the peoples of the area do need to ask themselves hard questions about how their societies are structured and why they have failed to develop in more promising ways. But I can understand too why many Arabs choose to heap much of the blame for their troubles on the West. It has sought to manipulate the Middle East for a century or more in order to control its own oil, and other, interests. I'm thinking, for example, of the carving up of the region in the aftermath of the First World War, the CIA-inspired coup in Iran in the fifties, the Suez Crisis, the French war in Algeria, and support for less than democratic regimes – not least that of Saddam Hussein, before he fell from favour. On top of this, the Arabs have watched their enemy, Israel, enjoy huge support from America, in particular. Moreover, they regard the lack of really serious, sustained Western pressure for an end to Israel's occupation of the Palestinian Territories as amounting to acquiescence – at the very least. And I haven't mentioned yet the current state of Iraq. I am not surprised, then, when I meet Arabs who are angry with the West. Nor am I surprised that some radical elements in the Middle East are harnessing that anger as they pursue their religious and political goals in keeping with their narrow, bleak interpretation of Islam. These were the kind of men who seized me. But I would argue that they are profoundly misguided, and that they are likely to bring their people new problems, rather than solutions. I feel, for instance, that my kidnapping damaged the reputation of Palestinians and their cause, and I think most people in Gaza would agree. And while I lay locked up and listening to my radio, I heard reports of extremist Islamist groups killing Muslims in large numbers in bombings and other attacks in Morocco, Algeria, Lebanon, Iraq, Pakistan and Afghanistan. I will not be surprised if groups like al-Qaeda manage to inflict more pain on the West in the years to come. But I think that they may in the end cause as much if not more damage and upheaval in their own societies.

Q: Your captors forced you to make a political statement on video. Tell us how you felt about that.

My guards came into my room at about three in the morning with a letter from the leader detailing what I had to say. I did attempt to obstruct the process. I made a very brief statement that I read in a halting manner, trying to make clear that I was speaking under duress. The guards took the tape away to show the leader, and he obviously didn't like what he saw. The next night the guards came back and said that I had to make a new, much fuller and more convincing statement. They said I had to 'co-operate if I wanted my freedom'. They held all the cards, and I had little choice.

My view was that any sensible person knows that video statements made by kidnap victims are always done under conditions of extraordinary duress. I don't imagine that many people take the words spoken very seriously.

On camera I talked of arrests and killings of Palestinians at the hands of Israeli forces. And of course during my time in Gaza I had seen much suffering, including the shooting of children, the demolition of many homes and the destruction of farmland. However, I wasn't able, in my video, to set the conflict in any context. The jihadis only wanted me to air their view.

For example, many Israeli army raids into Gaza are aimed at stopping the almost daily rocket fire. Palestinian militants launch crudely made devices that sometimes injure and occasionally kill people in Israeli towns and villages just across the border. This constitutes random bombardment of civilians, and it is clearly a war crime. The Israeli army's response often amounts to collective punishment, which is another kind of war crime.

But again, there is a wider context. The militants in Gaza often say that their attacks are made in response to Israeli army actions in the West Bank. For more than forty years the Israelis have sought to consolidate their occupation there and in East Jerusalem. The area of illegally built Jewish settlements has been relentlessly expanded for decades, and that process is continuing at this moment. The Israeli army controls the West Bank by means of hundreds of checkpoints, and pretty much every day it carries out raids and arrests. Palestinian militants and civilians are often killed.

But the conflict is not only about the occupation. Palestinian militant groups do talk about being committed – ultimately – to Israel's destruction. Those forces are very weak right now, and pose absolutely no immediate threat to Israel's survival. But if you know something of the history of the Jewish people, you can understand why, over the longer term, many Israelis view the attitude of the likes of the Hamas movement with deep concern.

However, if you want to try to understand the thinking of those Gazan militants firing rockets into Israel, it is worth bearing in mind that many of them come from refugee families. They lost their homes in what is now Israel when Arab armies were defeated in the war that they launched in 1948. And as those young Palestinians have grown up leading stunted, blighted lives in the camps of Gaza, they have had to watch Jews from all over the world come and settle on what used to be the lands of their fathers.

The more devout among those Jewish families have arrived from places such as Russia, France and Argentina believing passionately that in the days of Moses God gave them the right to live in the Land of Israel. And all Israel's Jewish immigrants would argue that they have a right to come and swell the numbers of their people, who have maintained some presence in the area since biblical times. But those Jewish religious and historical claims mean nothing to Palestinians. They see the rise of the Israeli state as having robbed them of their birthright in a land where a century ago their people were in the vast majority, and living peacefully. The Palestinians believe that God, history and justice are on their side.

This, then, is just some of the background to the conflict as I see it. Of course I was not able to give it in the video that my captors forced me to make. The jihadis were not very interested in the wider context, but then, unfortunately, neither are some Israelis.

Q: With regard to the conflict, is there any room for optimism in your view?

For a century or more, this has been a dispute over the control of the narrow strip of land that stretches from the River Jordan to the Mediterranean Sea. If the Israelis were to withdraw from every inch of occupied East Jerusalem and the West Bank, along with Gaza, the Palestinians would be left with about 22 per cent of that land. The Israelis would have 78 per cent. Every time you see an American president sit down with the two sides to talk peace, the question is largely about how much of that 22 per cent the Palestinians should be allowed to have – and under what conditions.

I tend to feel that the Israelis will never really give enough. I find it hard to envisage Israel ever stepping back and relinquishing sufficient control to allow the proposed tiny, fractured Palestinian state to flourish. And I don't see Israel being forced to give enough by its mighty ally, the United States, which, to the obvious despair of the Palestinians, is the referee in this fight.

Meanwhile, Hamas talks of being ready for an extended truce in return for an end to the occupation. But the likes of its supporters would not consider 22 per cent of the land to be enough to constitute a just long-term settlement of the conflict. I think that at least some Palestinian militants would be very hard to rein in – and in the poverty, hopelessness and oppression of the occupation, their ranks are only likely to grow. Set against all that, most people on both sides do want an end to the conflict – a settlement that might allow their children to live in peace and prosper. So perhaps there is some hope – 'God willing,' as they say in Palestine.

Q: *And what of your future? Given what you went through during your kidnapping, will you continue reporting from the Middle East?*

There was one night during my captivity when I listened on the radio to the BBC reporting claims that I had been executed. In the hours afterwards, I lay in the dark waiting to see if I might indeed be put to death. And I came to feel that I had pushed things in Gaza to the limit, and beyond. I felt that if I survived I would need to step back a little, and think hard about how and where I work, and how I lead my life. And I guess that is what I am doing now. I will stay in journalism – and, hopefully, the BBC – and perhaps I will eventually return to places like Gaza and Afghanistan and elsewhere. But the kidnap took quite a lot out of me, and for the moment, at least, I need to regain my strength a little. Just right now, it does feel good to be back in Britain – and very, very good to be free.

London
November 2007

Alan Johnston leaving Gaza and crossing into Israel after his ordeal
(Jack Guez/AFP/Getty Images)

AFGHANISTAN

Introduction

The term 'Third World' has rather fallen from favour
these days. But even when it was current I didn't feel
that it quite described Afghanistan properly. I used to
think of that country more as the Fourth World. Years
of Soviet occupation and civil war had left it the
poorest and most broken place that I had ever seen.

I arrived in Kabul soon after it had been stormed by
one of the more extraordinary political movements of
our time – the Taliban. They were my neighbours, and
I watched them start to try to run the smashed city.
Large tracts of it had been laid to waste as
Afghanistan's feuding mujaheddin factions had torn
at one another in and around the capital. But
reconstruction and providing homes and jobs weren't
really priorities for the Taliban; more important to
them was the re-ordering of society. They saw the city
as corrupt, a place that had gone along with the
communists during their time in power. In the
Taliban's eyes, Kabul had strayed far from what they
regarded as the true, austere path of Islam. The holy

warriors had emerged from the southern countryside to lay down God's law, as they believed it to be.

And so, at the start of 1997, I began to report on a rather surreal world. The Taliban were enforcing their bans on music and dancing, and musicians were hiding their instruments. The movement had a problem with any depiction of living creatures – animal or human. Films were burnt. Only much later did I meet a brave art lover who saved pictures in the national gallery by slipping in and painting over – in removable watercolours – shepherds and their sheep, and any other figures that might offend the mullahs. 'American-style' haircuts, short beards, high heels, paper bags, kites and much else were deemed unacceptable. And there were the bizarre press conferences to explain all this. At one, I remember listening to a spokesman for the Department for Promoting Virtue and Preventing Vice, who was discussing the list of outlawed items. I noticed that he included teddy bears, and without thinking I said that actually, they weren't banned. 'All right,' replied the spokesman, 'we'll ban them tonight!' I was appalled. I felt that Afghan kids had enough to cope with, without my getting their teddy bears outlawed by accident.

Much more serious in the coming of the new regime, of course, were the consequences for women. The

Taliban abhorred any mixing of the sexes outside the family, and so women were largely driven back to the home and under the all-concealing burkha. But in this, at least, the Taliban were not so far out of step with Afghan tradition. They were imposing the very conservative codes of the countryside on Kabul. Even before the Taliban arrived, the capital's female population was, by the standards of almost anywhere else, marginalised to an extraordinary degree. All this made reporting the views of women very hard. I barely saw an Afghan woman's face during my whole year in Kabul. At that time, to be caught interviewing a woman could have got me flung in prison, and it might have been very dangerous for her.

It's fair to say that in that first period of Taliban rule in Kabul, along with the resentment of their numerous edicts came a certain sense of relief. They had brought an austere calm and a new sense of security that had been very much lacking for a long time. There was, for example, a warlord who held sway on the main road into Kabul and kept a demented man chained up in a cave. The man was known as 'the human dog'. Any traveller who fell foul of the commander's fighters as they fleeced passers-by risked the horror of having the mad 'dog' unleashed, and being savaged by him. But the Taliban swept away all the checkpoints and petty warlords. They made it safe to travel anywhere in their territory. Soon, though, as they moved further north, they showed brutality and contempt for those who didn't share their own predominantly Pashtun ethnic roots, and who were linked with their enemies.

And there was already more trouble on the horizon for Afghanistan. I remember trying to get an interview with the mysterious, reclusive, one-eyed Taliban leader Mullah Omar. I spent three days lounging in the spring sunshine in his rose garden in Kandahar before finally having to accept that he wasn't going to speak to me – or any other Christian journalist. But in those days another visitor was always welcome at the warlord's court. His name was Osama Bin Laden.

For me, perhaps the best analysis of the Taliban and their associates came from a slightly older, French journalist. He had seen Pol Pot's Khmer Rouge in Cambodia, and he knew a bit about fanaticism and how it works. 'Beware,' he said, 'of those who believe that they are pure.'

Afghanistan's landscape is a thing of harsh beauty. The flanks of the mountains of the Hindu Kush rise above thin valleys, where the air and the soil are thinner still. For many Afghans, extracting a living from the rocky earth has been hard for centuries. This, and the wars that they've endured, have made them tougher than any people I've ever come across. But although theirs may be the poorest place on earth, I often found there a generosity of spirit that could put my own, much richer world to shame. I remember visiting an orphanage in Kabul. It was a winter's day, but there was no heat or light in the cold and gloomy dinning room. A huge, seemingly unwashed cook was working from a battered kitchen. Orphans were queuing to have a spoonful of some uneatable-looking brown goo slopped into their tin bowls. I watched a boy of about eight walk away with his miserable little meal. He was, I thought, at the very bottom of the heap. Does anyone, I wondered, have a harder start in life than an Afghan orphan? I, on the other hand, in material terms, had all that I could want. I had benefited from a fine education and I had a well-paid job in one of the world's richest societies. As I watched the boy sit down at a table, I reflected on how, in life's lottery, I had almost everything – and he had almost nothing. At that point the boy looked up. He smiled, and gestured at his plate. 'Eat with me!' he was saying, in a typically Afghan way. 'We can share it. There's enough for both of us.' I declined politely. I felt that, in my time, I had eaten enough.

FIRST IMPRESSIONS

The warring factions in Afghanistan were continuing
to confront each other in the Hindu Kush
mountains as Alan arrived in Kabul. These were his
initial impressions of the country, its people and the
war. (5 April 1997)

AT THE TOP OF THE KHYBER PASS stand two high blue gates. The Pakistani frontier guards unchained them and swung them open to reveal Afghanistan beyond. This was one of the world's poorest countries before it endured invasion and devastation by the Soviet army, and Afghanistan gets poorer as the civil war drags on. There have now been eighteen years of fighting.

At the frontier you have an immediate sense of this poverty. At what is Afghanistan's main gateway, passport officials operate in the cold and gloom of a hut without electricity. Through the window in sunlight on the far side of the valley there are camels tethered near nomad tents. There are more camels, long lines of them, being led by traders along the rutted road running from the frontier to Kabul. The highway leads you through a desert landscape; great expanses of stones stretch away to bare mountainsides, a place without trees where the only colours are shades of brown, until you reach the green of the valley around Jalalabad. In the villages heavily veiled women go between the high walls of the houses built of mud, men work the fields without modern machines and there's barely a trace of the late twentieth century.

In recent months an army has swept up this same road. The purist Islamist Taliban movement stormed Kabul in September and sent shock waves far beyond the mountains of Afghanistan. An outside world gearing up for the twenty-first century looked on with some astonishment as the Taliban revealed their contempt for much that is central to modern Western life. By decree women were ordered to go entirely covered at all times outside their homes, and they've been barred from education and employment. Television, music and dancing have all been banned. The Taliban believe that theirs is the army of God and that their mission is to restore what they regard as Islamic purity to Afghan society.

Their enemies are the mujaheddin guerrilla groups that defeated the Soviet army. The Taliban say the old guerrilla leaders and their allies have become corrupted and must be crushed. For their part, those opposing the Taliban say the movement is no more than a force created by elements in Pakistan to keep Afghanistan unstable.

At the moment the Taliban army is in what its leaders call the trenches of righteousness on front lines north of Kabul. There you find the Taliban waging their warfare from the back of Japanese pick-up trucks, which form a kind of cavalry in this war in the Hindu Kush mountains. The trucks fly the Taliban flag – white to symbolise purity – and to the back of each cab is lashed a cluster of rocket-propelled grenades. The fighters themselves are packed into the open backs of the trucks, wrapped in flapping brown shawls and hanging on as their vehicles pound along the smashed roads. Many wear shiny black turbans, some have traditional thick black make-up around their eyes, and with their beards and weapons they look every bit as forbidding as you might expect of Afghan holy warriors. Also on the roads near the front are the refugees; more than 100,000 have streamed down the highway to Kabul. They've either fled the fighting or been expelled from their homes by the advancing Taliban. Most go crammed into some of the oldest, most decrepit buses you have ever seen. The poorest walk. The women float along, shrouded in the flowing blue burkha, the Islamic dress that covers the wearer completely from head to foot. Through a small patch of gauze sewn into the fabric around their eyes the women peer out at deserted villages and wrecked farms.

The bleakest scene lay on the Salang highway, which slices through the Hindu Kush. The road connects northern and southern Afghanistan and it would be a vital economic link had it not been sabotaged by the retreating forces of the north. Just back from a blown-up bridge one more family of refugees was packing its belongings into a bus. Just yards away a soldier lay dead, his brains in the snow beside him. As the refugees went on loading their bus there was heaving and shouting and children milled about. After eighteen years of war Afghanistan is a place where bodies in the snow can go almost unnoticed.

NO CINEMA IN
SOROBI

The Taliban's series of laws and prohibitions
astounded the outside world. The decrees were
making a huge difference to life in the capital, but in
other parts of the country little was changing.
(16 April 1997)

WESTERN POLITICIANS MIGHT BE OBSESSED by popularity ratings, but not the Taliban. Last month on the eve of the traditional, much-loved Afghan New Year festivities, they cancelled the celebrations. They said the ancient festival was un-Islamic. And the Taliban enforce their rules unbendingly.

Women have to cover themselves entirely. If they leave their eyes showing in Kabul they risk a public beating. You now never see a woman's face on the city's streets. Men must grow their beards in a style that the Taliban regard as appropriately Islamic. At the interior ministry the other morning I found that most of the officials were absent. They'd been called away for examination by a team of beard inspectors. At least a hundred civil servants had been sacked for trimming their facial hair. Unsurprisingly you now see beards in Kabul getting longer by the day.

Music has been declared un-Islamic and these days it's never heard in public. The only exception is the hymns the Taliban fighters like to play in the trucks that they drive to the front lines. The songs dwell on bleak

themes, like martyrdom, and they're always sung by a
lone male unaccompanied by instruments. If fighters
spot a music cassette in a car they will confiscate and
smash it. Clumps of cassette tape, like glistening
entrails, decorate almost every Taliban checkpoint.

The Taliban mindset was forged in the religious
schools, the madrasahs of the Afghan-Pakistan
frontier region. Years of devotion and scholarship have
left the Taliban's clerical leaders, the mullahs, with an
absolute belief that only rigorous adherence to their
interpretation of Islam is acceptable. In Kabul you find
the morality police at the Department for Promoting
Virtue and Preventing Vice. The department's chief,
Mullah Rafiullah Muhazeen, sees the West as a place
where individual freedoms have been allowed to run
riot. He points to the adultery admitted to by Diana,
Princess of Wales, as an illustration of Western
society's rottenness. Mullah Muhazeen says he's
watched for nearly half a century as Afghans have been
led away from the Islamic path by damaging foreign
ideas. For Mullah Muhazeen it is the cities that are the
problem. It's there that the polluting Western and
Soviet influences took hold, it's there that Afghan
women shed the veil and began to dress in ways that
might attract a man's attention. Mullah Muhazeen
says he's surprised that there are Afghan husbands
who used to allow their wives to go on their own to sit

in an office in the presence of another man. How, the mullah asked, could such a husband still regard that woman as his wife at the end of the working day? It seems that the Taliban are determined to take Kabul by the scruff of the neck and lead it back to an imagined lost purity.

Of course many sophisticated Afghan urbanites are aghast at the Taliban approach. They resent the intrusions into the smallest details of their lives and they fear that their country is being led into a gathering cultural and intellectual darkness.

But the Taliban have not only brought their harsh interpretation of Islam, they've also brought a calm and order that Afghans have not known for nearly twenty years. They've disarmed countless groups of gunmen and bandits that used to plague the more than two-thirds of Afghanistan that the Taliban have captured. Many city people may be contemptuous of the Taliban but most appreciate the new sense of security, and in the countryside the Taliban's attitudes towards women and beards and cinemas have changed nothing. In large areas of Afghanistan, country people have always lived by the values that the Taliban are now forcing on Kabul.

In the small country town of Sorobi I found the Taliban governor taking his afternoon sleep on the floor of his bare office. He woke and offered me tea. I asked him how rigorously he imposed the regulations on women's dress. He said he didn't have to impose them. He said that Sorobi was a very traditional place and that the town's women almost never left their homes. When they did, he said, they wouldn't dream of going unveiled. I asked the governor if he had prohibited girls from going to school. He said that Sorobi girls had never been educated. I didn't need to ask if the Taliban had shut the cinema in Sorobi. There is no cinema in Sorobi.

TREACHERY AND THE TALIBAN

The Afghan month of Jawzaa turned out to be a momentous and violent one. There was a revolt in the ranks of the anti-Taliban alliance in the north of the country with several important generals rebelling and switching sides to the Taliban camp, and there was fierce fighting in the north's regional capital, Mazar-i-Sharif. (7 July 1997)

DRAMATIC MILITARY AND POLITICAL CHANGE in Afghanistan rarely comes purely through battlefield victories. Much more often change comes in the wake of a sudden shift of allegiance. And last month there was such a shift. Key generals in the northern anti-Taliban alliance rebelled and joined the Taliban. Together rebel troops and Taliban fighters occupied the northern capital, Mazar-i-Sharif. The Taliban appeared close to asserting their authority over the whole country.

Taliban rule comes with an austere interpretation of Islam. The Taliban regard music, dancing, television and the cinema as un-Islamic and prohibit them. Women can be flogged for failing to cover themselves entirely in public and females are barred from almost any job that might bring them into contact with men. Many educated Afghans in the cities dread the prospect of protracted rule by Taliban leaders, who are determined to march the country back to what they regard as a lost age of Islamic purity. But set against this, the Taliban have developed a reputation for restoring order. They've disarmed countless petty commanders and bands of gunmen who made large areas of Afghanistan dangerous and chaotic for years.

Whichever way you might view the Taliban, it seemed that their new alliance in the north, coupled with possible talks with other anti-Taliban groups, might finally bring nearly two decades of war to an end.

On the front line in the Hindu Kush mountains in the centre of the country it was easy to begin to believe that peace was coming. One of the main anti-Taliban commanders, Baseer Salangi, emerged from talks to tell hundreds of ecstatic Taliban fighters that he too was joining their camp. Fighters piled on tanks and trucks roared their approval and blared their horns. They shouted their battle cry: '*Allahu Akbar*' – God is great. '*Allahu Akbar*,' Commander Salangi shouted back.

Later I saw Taliban fighters forget their ban on dancing to go into a slow stamping, chanting dance of delight. I remember following a pick-up truck on the highway that winds through the Hindu Kush. In the open back sat a Taliban fighter and a guerrilla from the opposition forces. Just hours ago they were enemies, but as the pick-up went racing round the mountain bends they laughed and laughed and laughed together.

The Taliban troops poured through the Hindu Kush into the territory of the opposition Northern Alliance. But their column only got as far as the town of Pul-i-Khumri, before there came staggering news from further north. The Taliban's new alliance with the rebel generals had collapsed. Large numbers of Taliban lay dead in the streets of Mazar-i-Sharif and their surviving comrades were being driven out of the north. The Taliban column in Pul-i-Khumri found its route back south through the mountains suddenly cut off, and opposition forces quickly surrounded the town.

Later, Commander Baseer Salangi announced that his defection had just been a trick to lure Taliban troops northwards into the Pul-i-Khumri trap. And so the people of Pul-i-Khumri town, and us handful of journalists among them, began to ask ourselves the questions that anyone in a siege must ask. How long, we wondered, could the Taliban hold out? Would it be days or weeks or months? How would it end? Perhaps there'd be a sudden Taliban collapse and a mad, dangerous guns-blazing charge into Pul-i-Khumri by their enemies. Would the victorious troops loot the town? Or would the Taliban fight for every house, every basement? If that happened, would the attackers stand back and pound Pul-i-Khumri to rubble?

As we wondered and waited and sifted the rumours, the guns rumbled on the front lines north and south of the town. We journalists didn't stay for the final act. We heard it might be possible to leave north-eastwards on a road where there was a front line of sorts, but no fighting yet. Later, as we circled round to see the siege of Pul-i-Khumri from the attacking side, we found that the town had fallen a few hours before. As it turned out there'd been no street fighting, no bombardment, no looting and almost no drama. The Taliban had simply slipped away in the night, tactically retreating to fight another day in the farmland north-east of Pul-i-Khumri. The attacking forces had walked in, barely firing a shot. The siege was over.

In the main street we met a driver we knew. Like many Pul-i-Khumri men, while the Taliban held the town, he'd started growing the beard that the Taliban insist all Muslim men must wear. But they were gone now, and the driver stood laughing and slapping his shiny, smooth cheeks – he'd already shaved.

THE COMMISSIONER VISITS

The visit by the European Union's Commissioner for Humanitarian Affairs may have been intended to bridge the gap between Taliban-controlled Afghanistan and Europe, but it turned into a spectacular fiasco. (13 October 1997)

THE VISIT OF THE European Union's Commissioner for Humanitarian Affairs, Emma Bonino, was to be the diplomatic event of the year. She was by far the highest-ranking political figure to come since the Taliban captured Kabul a year ago. At the same time the EU is Afghanistan's biggest single aid donor. But most importantly Ms Bonino came with human rights on her mind and the Taliban record is contentious in the extreme.

The mullahs of the Taliban and Ms Bonino inhabit different political planets. Her roots are in Italy's radical libertarian fringe; Ms Bonino's successful pro-abortion campaign involved her imprisonment and a hunger strike. The Pope branded her a witch during her battle to reform Italian divorce law. Ms Bonino has been described as a firebrand who is very much at home in the thick of a fight.

Her visit to the land of the Taliban always looked likely to be controversial but nobody was prepared for the scale of the rumpus. Word spread fast across Kabul that the Bonino party had run into some kind of big trouble. For a while the high-level Euro delegation was simply missing. Then over the walkie-talkie network – which substitutes for a phone system in Kabul – came a message that the Bonino team had been detained at District One police station in the heart of the bazaar. It was hard to believe that the Taliban had actually arrested the most important person to visit Kabul since their rule here began.

But there she was, sheltering in the shade of a tree in the station courtyard. Her Taliban guards in their turbans, baggy robes and sandals, with their rifles slung over their shoulders, stepped in and explained. For them it was an open and shut case. The Bonino group, which included three television crews, had been caught filming during a visit to a hospital. The Taliban strictly prohibit filming of all living creatures on religious grounds. The guards said they were treating Ms Bonino well, pointing out that they'd even given her a Pepsi.

A few hours later a furious Ms Bonino told a different story as she was freed and emerged from the shade of her tree into a blaze of international publicity. She described traumatic scenes as the Taliban police moved in during her hospital tour. She said she'd been threatened with a Kalashnikov rifle and at one point the European commissioner had had to wrestle to hang on to the bag she was carrying. Members of her party were struck as the excitement rose. Ms Bonino talked of having sampled something of what she called the Taliban's reign of terror and then made off for neighbouring Pakistan as she was scheduled to do.

As the dust settled, the Taliban revealed themselves to be profoundly unimpressed and even less apologetic. Ms Bonino, they said, had brought her troubles on herself. Her team had broken the law. They had failed to respect local customs and breached very widely publicised rules forbidding filming. Ms Bonino's claim to have been threatened with a Kalashnikov carried little weight in the robust world of the Taliban. A spokesman said the commissioner had neither been shot at nor struck with a rifle and could not therefore claim to have been threatened. Neither had Ms Bonino been thrown in jail or put in chains; the spokesman said the Italian lady had blown the matter out of all proportion.

But in fact the whole affair was damaging in that it had confirmed the worst prejudices of both sides. The Bonino people had indeed demonstrated scant regard for local regulations. The fact that the filming had gone on in a women's hospital particularly irritated the authorities. The Taliban on the other hand had demonstrated their genius for attracting the most appalling kind of publicity; detaining a very important visitor on a humanitarian mission was clumsy in the extreme.

What little chance there might have been of the Bonino visit marking the start of a dialogue between Europe and the Taliban was lost in the arrest and the welter of mutual recriminations. The visit was a fiasco that served only to entrench differences and widen the chasm across which the Taliban and their Western critics glower at one another.

FEARS FOR THE BUDDHAS

There was growing concern about the state of one of Asia's great archaeological treasures, the Buddhas of Bamiyan. The huge figures, carved into a cliff face, overlooked a valley in the heart of the Hindu Kush mountains. The statues were of great historical significance and there were fears that they could be damaged, destroyed even, in the civil war raging around them. (15 December 1997)

CENTRAL AFGHANISTAN THRIVED in the days of the Silk Road. Camel caravans criss-crossed the region as they traded between the Roman Empire, China and India. And as they journeyed through the Hindu Kush mountains they came upon Bamiyan, one of the wonders of the ancient world. This heart of the now-forgotten Kingdom of Kushan had been glorified by two colossal Buddha statues. They were carved into a cliff in the mountains that tower over the valley of Bamiyan.

One of the statues stands as high as a ten-storey building and has been described as the most remarkable representation of the Buddha anywhere in the world. These vast statues were painted in gold and other colours and they were decked in dazzling ornaments. All around there was a synthesis of Greek, Persian and Central and South Asian art. There were countless rich frescoes. On one cave wall there were images of Buddhas in maroon robes strolling in fields of flowers. In another place milk-white horses drew the Sun God's golden chariot through a dark-blue sky.

There were ten monasteries built into the cliff, there were yellow-robed monks, there were pilgrims, festivals, fluttering pennants and silken canopies.

Today, Bamiyan is a very much more austere place. The monks and the pilgrims went many centuries ago when Islam came to the Hindu Kush. For a time the 1960s hippy trail passed this way and there were tourists, but they too have gone. Bamiyan is immersed so deep in Afghanistan's war that even the great stone Buddhas have been drawn into the conflict.

The Bamiyan region is the stronghold of the Hezb-i-Wahdat, the main faction representing the Shi'a Muslims of the centre of the country. Hezb-i-Wahdat is one of the pillars of the alliance that opposes the purist, Islamist Taliban movement. During the summer, Taliban forces advanced down the valley towards Bamiyan town. In the Islamic fervour of the march, a Taliban commander said that when he broke through and took the town, he would blow up its famous statues. In his eyes, they were offensive and sacrilegious – the idols of infidels.

It wasn't the first time that Bamiyan's Buddhas had faced the wrath of an iconoclastic soldier. Eleven centuries ago the Muslim warrior Yaqoub rampaged through the area. He destroyed Buddhist temples and reportedly seized fifty idols in gold and silver. And on the frescoes the faces of many Buddha figures have been chiselled out by those intent on destroying what they regarded as the soul force of the idol.

News of the Taliban commander's threat this summer to renew this kind of destruction spread fast. There was alarm across the Buddhist world and the United Nations expressed grave concern. Later the Taliban leadership assured the international community that no harm would come to the statues.

In the event the Taliban were defeated and driven back. Bamiyan and the Buddhas remain firmly under the control of the forces of Hezb-i-Wahdat. But they too have given the archaeologists cause to worry. For a time they stored large amounts of ammunition in ancient caves built into the cliff at the feet of the largest of the two Buddhas. This giant figure of tremendous historical significance was effectively standing on a mound of explosives.

But the local authorities are aware that the Buddhist complex is important. They know that it'll be a major tourist attraction again once peace finally comes. They've been persuaded to remove the ammunition stockpile, but they're still using the caves to store sackloads of wheat. Every day lorries loading and unloading manoeuvre right at the Buddha's feet. They're sending damaging fumes and vibrations up his giant frame to the fragile frescoes that adorn the area around his head. And conservationists continue to be deeply concerned by military activity in the general area of the statue complex, which could at some point attract potentially devastating fighting.

Quite recently, during a Taliban air raid, a jet dropped a bomb just a hundred metres from the largest Buddha. And the war is bringing destruction of a different kind to the warren of hundreds of caves that used to house the monasteries and their monks. Refugees who have fled areas of fighting in other parts of Afghanistan have moved into the maze of grottos. The whole cliff face is alive with the activity of these modern cave people.

I met a man called Janat Mir who was building a wall and a door for the front of the cave which shelters his numerous children. Their home near Kabul was smashed in an artillery strike which also killed Janat Mir's father. The cave is now all they have. But just by their presence, the family and its donkey, like the other cave dwellers, are of course doing damage to what is one of the world's great archaeological sites.

The whole extraordinary, ancient Buddhist complex is in desperate need of proper preservation. It needs management and control to prevent it being ruined by soldiers or refugees or thieves who might loot what remains of the frescoes. But of course in poverty-stricken central Afghanistan there aren't anything like the necessary resources or archaeological know-how to care properly for the giant Buddhas of Bamiyan. The site is being degraded day by day. Local people who care for the complex are appealing to the Buddhist world in particular and to what they call the culture-loving countries of the West to come forward. They're looking to the outside world to help, no matter how great the obstacles posed by the Afghan war.

DESTRUCTION OF THE BUDDHAS

There was an international outcry when the Taliban
destroyed the twin Buddhas of Bamiyan.
(22 November 2003)

I REMEMBER CLIMBING THE CLIFF at Bamiyan years ago. High on the rock face the path led you into a low, dark tunnel. It took you round to a ledge where you could almost have reached out and touched the head of the Giant Buddha, a wonder of the ancient world, and the pride of Bamiyan. But to make the same climb today is a much, much sadder experience. The colossal statue is gone, a casualty of the Taliban, who saw it as nothing more than a shrine for infidels. When you reach that ledge at the end of the tunnel now, there's nothing; just a great void, and a pile of broken stones more than fifty metres down.

But you are at least left with the scene that the Buddha gazed on for 1,500 years: the mud-built homes and the pale fields of the valley of Bamiyan. And all around, in the thin, cold air ... are the slopes and jagged ridges of the Hindu Kush, the heart of Afghanistan.

The Taliban's destruction of the Buddhas was condemned around the world, but the suffering of Bamiyan's people has gone almost unnoticed beyond the valley. For years the Taliban battled to subdue the

Hazaras, the main ethnic group in the central mountains. Down through history the Hazara people have endured the status of an underclass in Afghanistan, and the Taliban held them in special contempt. The Hazaras are of the Shi'ite branch of Islam, whereas the Taliban, like most Afghans, are drawn from the Sunni sect of the faith. In one area of the mountains nearly 5,000 homes and shops were burnt down in just two days. Over the years, the Taliban put to death at least 1,200 Hazaras. Four mass graves were found in Bamiyan town alone, and more may well be unearthed.

But life in the valley is moving on again. I could have walked its country roads all day and I wouldn't have seen a warlord's checkpoint or even a gunman. Instead I saw farmhouses, which had been destroyed by the Taliban, now standing rebuilt and surrounded by trees turning golden with the autumn. Down in a clearing in the woods, in a mud shack built over a stream, a stone wheel – spinning and humming – was milling the wheat harvest. I watched the old miller himself step out to take a break in the sunshine, his Afghan robes and the folds in his turban covered in the fine white flour dust that hung in the air. It was all a long way from the Afghanistan that the world sees, a land of guerrilla fighters and religious fanatics. And it was easy to feel, down by the old mill-house, that Bamiyan has found some of the peace for which it has longed for more than twenty years.

But these mountains are the poorest part of one of the world's poorest countries. There just isn't enough good soil to farm in the narrow valleys, and for generations the Hazara people have been forced to leave to try to make a hard living in Kabul, or even find work in the factories of faraway Iranian cities, like Shiraz and Isfahan.

The only great asset that Bamiyan had was the site of the Buddha statues, which presented huge possibilities in terms of one day attracting tourists and their dollars. Of course the Taliban crippled that potential when they destroyed the giant Buddhas. But even now this beautiful place retains a certain power. All along the rock face, which is tinged a reddish colour, there are caves and chambers cut into the sandstone. These would have served as prayer halls and monasteries during Bamiyan's golden age. At that time Buddhist pilgrims would have travelled down the Silk Road trade route to worship at what was then a great centre of faith and learning. Merchant caravans would also have been passing through Bamiyan. Their camels would have been loaded with spices and cloths and precious stones from China and the cities on the Ganges and some of their merchandise would have been destined to go as far as the gates of ancient Rome. We're told that at festival times the traders would have mingled with yellow-robed monks beneath silken canopies. Towering serenely over the whole scene would have been the great Buddhas; festooned with offerings and so brightly painted that according to one traveller, they 'dazzled the eye'. And, intriguingly, the best written account of seventh-century Bamiyan talks not just of two giant Buddhas, but three.

According to the record, the third Buddha, the missing Buddha, wasn't standing. He lay sleeping. If he exists, he has escaped the fury of the Taliban, but then, where could he be now? Some experts believe that a landslide may have covered him long ago, or that he lies slumbering in some forgotten chamber concealed deep in the cliff face. Is it just possible that in the years to come the archaeologists, who are already working on the site, will unearth the missing Buddha? It would surely be one of the great finds of our time, and the best possible response to those Taliban soldiers who cheered as they dynamited the gentle giants of Bamiyan.

A PICNIC WITH
GENERAL DOSTUM

In the days after the 9/11 attacks in the United
States, the Americans were leading an operation
to drive the Taliban from power. At the same
time, in the north of the country, one of
Afghanistan's most formidable warlords, General
Abdur Rashid Dostum, was plotting to recapture
his Mazar-i-Sharif stronghold. Alan had met the
general four years earlier. (3 November 2001)

EARLY ONE MORNING in the spring of 1997, I was standing on the Soviet-made airstrip outside Mazar-i-Sharif. Beyond the tarmac, the flat steppe land of Central Asia gave way to a line of mountains, a spur of the Hindu Kush range. Off to the left sat a dilapidated old military helicopter that looked badly in need of repair. I asked a militia officer where the helicopter was that was supposed to take me to the front line. Disturbingly, he just pointed at the machine that looked badly in need of repair.

Eventually, the pilot coaxed the clattering, shuddering contraption into the air and we were off, low over the steppe on our way to the battleground, and an appointment with General Abdur Rashid Dostum. During the Soviet occupation the general started his career on the communist side of the war as a security officer in a factory. But he quickly expanded his horizons. He transformed his security unit into a fighting force drawn from his own Uzbek ethnic group, which dominates this part of northern Afghanistan. Soon his men were being used by the communist government as shock troops against the mujaheddin guerrillas. They were sent to do their brutal business in areas where the hold of the regime was most tenuous. And when General Dostum eventually switched sides, and allied himself with the guerrillas, it spelt the end of the communist government in Kabul.

By the time that I'd climbed aboard that helicopter in 1997, the war had brought the army of the Taliban movement to the borders of General Dostum's northern stronghold. But that spring morning the word was that his militia had made some advances on the long front line in the rolling hills of Badghis province.

The helicopter put us down close to the front. The place bustled with General Dostum's fighters, many in traditional Uzbek dress: tightly bound turbans and long padded coats for keeping out the icy winds of the steppe. Far away, across a plain, a column of armed horsemen was making its way down a hillside. They hit the flat ground and broke into a canter. This was Uzbek cavalry, perhaps a hundred-strong, surging towards us, dust rising from the pounding hooves. And there at the centre of the line, on a white charger, rode General Dostum himself.

As the riders reached us they reined in hard. There was a great neighing of horses and stamping of hooves. We were engulfed in dust, and the gathered soldiers roared in salute of their commander-in-chief. The warlord dismounted and strode towards me, a huge man in a turban, his Uzbek jacket reaching down to his riding boots, and in his hand he carried a whip. He was orchestrating what amounted to a grandiose photo opportunity. His fighters had had some success and he wanted to make sure that the BBC and the outside world knew about it. In his deep, booming voice he joked with his troops and gave a running commentary as he strode down a line of captured Taliban vehicles. The general glowered briefly at a forlorn group of six Taliban prisoners of war.

He lined up his senior officers and introduced them to me one by one. He'd been angered by some report in the media that his generals had been absent from the front. He wanted to make the point that they were, in fact, all there and putting in a good day's work. Next a string of jeeps took us rocketing up a hillside. At the summit, arrangements had been made for a picnic like no other. There were carpets and cushions spread on the grass, and there was chicken and rice and fruit and nuts. The guns on the front line were silent, and as we ate and drank we gazed at the hills, which turned blue in the distance as they rose and fell towards Iran. The general talked of politics and war, and at one stage he pointed with a chicken bone at a peak off to the left and said: 'See that mountain – the one with the snow on it? Well, I captured it three days ago.'

As it turned out, one of the commanders lounging with us on the cushions at that picnic betrayed General Dostum a few months later. It was the kind of act of grand treachery that is very much a part of Afghan warfare. General Dostum lost his front line in the hills of Badghis and soon the whole of his northern stronghold was gone. The general endured a brief exile in Turkey, but stormed back within months to retake his lands. In another stunning reversal he lost them once more to the Taliban the next year. And Mazar-i-Sharif could be about to fall yet again. General Dostum is back in the north, and he is determined to drive the Taliban from Mazar one last time. He has complained that he lacks heavy weaponry. He is reported to be using riders armed with Kalashnikovs, just like the cavalry that I saw four years ago, before that picnic on the Badghis front.

So here we are, at the start of the twenty-first century, and Mazar-i-Sharif is still locked in a scene that could be drawn from the darkest passages in Central Asia's history. Armed horsemen laying siege to a city on the steppe; it is a drama in which Genghis Khan would have felt at home.

PROFESSOR ON THE FRONT LINE

In the days after the fall of the Taliban, Kabul's once well-known university was haunted by memories of happier days. (11 December 2001)

AN OLD KABUL UNIVERSITY PROFESSOR I know, a tall, thin man with a greying beard, loves to talk of the years when he was a student on the campus. These were among Afghanistan's last years of peace, and the best days of the professor's life. The university was one of Asia's finest. The elite of Afghanistan passed through its doors. The campus was built mostly with American money; and British and French academics taught in faculty buildings that were linked by gardens and tree-lined avenues. The setting was perfect and the students had first-class libraries, laboratories – everything they could possibly need.

But the country beyond the university was one of the world's most backward. The fine young minds gathered on the campus were hungry for ideas that might bring rapid change. Some looked to Soviet-style communism for a solution. Others were drawn to China and Maoism and still others believed that the answers lay in political Islam. My professor friend watched as his university was gradually gripped by powerful, competing, foreign ideas that would eventually destroy both it and Afghanistan.

There were demonstrations and fights and eventually some deaths on campus. And after the April revolution brought a communist regime to power in 1978 it persecuted its Islamist enemies at the university. The professor said goodbye to Western academic friends and the Russians moved in.

But the university's troubles really began after the mujaheddin guerrillas captured Kabul in the spring of 1992. As factions that now make up the Northern Alliance fought between themselves, the campus became a battlefield.

There was huge destruction as fighters held out in the different faculties and looted everything worth taking. An acquaintance of the professor who tried to stop the ransacking of the main library was beaten so badly that he died a few days later. Books were carted off for sale or burnt to keep the fighters warm through the winter.

Laboratory equipment was smashed and sold for scrap. Landmines were strewn in the campus gardens, and dead bodies stuffed down wells.

There were surreal moments too: the old professor remembers watching a fighter ride a donkey out of the rector's office. When he was asked what he was doing, the fighter said that the donkey belonged to the enemy and that he'd just arrested it. The professor was witnessing the ruin of the place in which he'd spent his youth and all of his working life; and at the same time the fighting had spread to his nearby home.

Militiamen set up a machine gun on the roof of his house and the professor remembers watching their legs shake with fear as they fired deafening bursts at the hill behind the university. He could take it no more and abandoned his home to the fighters. They looted everything but not before he'd returned to make one mad effort to save some of his academic books, a bid to preserve something from a more sane past. He loaded the volumes on to a little cart and as he ran he heard the bullets whistle through the air above him.

The university had barely begun to recover from the impact of the fighting when the Taliban took control of Kabul and the campus along with it five years ago. In line with their almost total ban on female education, women were barred from all faculties. The university's academic range was drastically narrowed. The professor remembers going to a seminar on war-related trauma at which the young Taliban Minister of Higher Education dismissed the science of psychology as useless. He told the audience that all the answers lay in the Koran.

The Taliban have gone now, and so have the landmines. But strolling through the gardens you still see everywhere the signs of destruction from the time that the university was a front line. There's been no water or electricity on the campus for nearly ten years. Ageing professors like my friend sit in freezing offices. They haven't been paid their tiny wages for five months. There are no phones, no computers and no worthwhile books. Worst of all there are very few students. Afghanistan's devastated school system isn't producing enough young people fit to go on to university and fewer still can afford to. The Education Faculty managed to produce just one teacher last year. The whole university is on its knees, haunted by memories of a happier past. But for a few weeks now, there's been talk of peace in Afghanistan. After all that's happened it seems almost too much to hope for.

But you can see in his eyes that my friend the professor can't help wondering if just maybe something of the old days will return. That if Afghanistan can just hold to the course of peace, maybe the brightest and the best young Afghans will be back, aspiring to great things in a better country.

CENTRAL ASIA

Introduction

For about seventy years, Central Asia was buried and forgotten in the depths of the Soviet Union. The desert and steppe lands that sweep from Mongolia to the shores of the Caspian Sea were largely out of bounds to foreigners. We in the West heard almost nothing about the world of the Kazakh, Kyrgyz, Uzbek, Tajik and Turkmen peoples. To us they were lost in a remote, mysterious, communist back of beyond. But all that changed with the Soviet Union's sudden collapse. And as the region emerged from the rubble of Moscow's broken empire, I was lucky enough to be sent to explore it.

This was, of course, the land of the old Silk Road, the trails followed by the camel caravans that carried merchandise through the Mountains of Heaven and over the great grasslands on the route between China and the Roman Empire. My journeys tended to be a little less romantic. Often I'd go rattling across the steppe in the back of a taxi or aboard a bus. But many of the destinations were magical: the city of

Samarkand, or Bukhara, or the Pamir mountains, or
the dying Aral Sea. Yaks and nomads, secret policemen
and drunken soldiers, vodka and steaming piles of
rice, shady tea houses and the sun catching the snow
on peaks that floated above the steppe: you don't easily
forget Central Asia.

And so for two years, based in Uzbekistan's capital,
Tashkent, I watched five brand-new Muslim nations
try to get to their feet. No wonder it was a struggle.

The Central Asians hadn't fought for their freedom –
rather, they had it thrust upon them. Poorer outposts,
like Tajikistan, had benefited financially at least from
the Soviet Union, and across the region people quickly
began to lament the passing of its certainties. Soon
newly independent Tajikistan and its neighbours were
running into serious economic trouble. People would
tell you that they used to have one job and two holidays
a year, but now they were forced to take two jobs if
they could find them – and there would be no more
holidays.

While Moscow's writ still ran, ethnic and religious
tensions were stifled. But in some parts, and in
different ways, they came to the fore with the end of
Soviet rule. Tens of thousands of people died in the
civil war in Tajikistan. And on one of the world's most
remote battlefronts, high in the Pamir mountains, and

down on the banks of the river that marked the Afghan frontier, I found Islamist guerrillas confronting the Russian soldiers who backed the Tajik government.

Everywhere it was the region's old communist leadership, the grey men of the Soviet past, who quickly made it clear that they weren't about to step aside. They were determined to inherit the new republics. I remember asking the Uzbek leader, Islam Karimov, how he could now pass himself off as an Uzbek nationalist when he had devoted all the decades of his career to the Soviet system that had denied Uzbeks any possibility of truly independent national expression. He answered that it sometimes takes time to find the correct path in political life. During that period Mr Karimov was busy breaking the last vestiges of the democratic opposition. He has gone on to consolidate what is one of the world's most repressive regimes as his secret police pursue his Islamist and other enemies. A United Nations report has described torture as being 'systematic' in Uzbek prisons.

Next door, in Turkmenistan, I watched the development of one of the world's most ludicrous cults of personality. At the time, a pudgy-faced, former Soviet Communist Party boss, Saparmurat Niyazov, had the country by the scruff of the neck, and was passing himself off almost as some sort of Turkmen messiah. Whole cities, the month of January and even a meteor were named in his honour. Meanwhile schoolchildren were being forced to learn by heart the spiritual guide that the great man had written.

Democracy never played a part in Central Asia's past, and I fear that it will be a long time before it is allowed to really catch fire on the steppe.

All of that, the grim politics, the Tajik war and the wretched economics, I covered in hundreds of hard news despatches. But when I look through the files, it was issues of identity that seemed to occupy me when I wrote for *From Our Own Correspondent*. The peoples of the region were no longer being shaped in the Soviet image. Suddenly they were free to make their own way, but they seemed uncertain as to exactly which direction to take. How much should they choose to keep of the Soviet legacy? To what extent, and in what way, should their Turkic roots and Islamic heritage be revived? As they sought to take their place in the world, they were looking to their pre-Soviet past to find out who they were, and what kind of people they might become.

In the despatches that follow, then, is just a little of what I saw – in the words of the poem, 'on the golden road to Samarkand'.

THE TREASURES OF SAMARKAND

Efforts to restore the great architectural treasures of the Silk Road city of Samarkand were quickening. The restoration work that had been going on for decades almost ground to a halt in the last years of Soviet rule. But newly independent Uzbekistan, as it sought a national identity, was resurrecting the glories of the region's past. The restoration process was also aimed at capitalising on the Silk Road and Samarkand's potential to become one of Asia's great tourist attractions. (13 October 1993)

WHEN ALEXANDER THE GREAT came upon
Samarkand, or Maracanda as it was then, it was
already hundreds of years old. He said everything he
had heard about it was true but that it was more
beautiful than he could ever have imagined. His Greek
followers are said to have built a great temple, and
archaeologists are searching for it today. As they dug
down they came across a black layer in the soil. It
turned out to be the ash that was all that was left of
Maracanda after Genghis Khan's Mongols burnt it to
the ground.

Later, the great fourteenth-century conqueror
Tamerlane built his capital on the site. Samarkand
became the centre of an empire stretching from India
to the Mediterranean. Tales of Tamerlane's cruelty
caught the West's imagination. For example, in the
Persian city of Isfahan, he made a pyramid out of the
skulls of 4,000 of his enemies. But Tamerlane was also
an artistic visionary and he made his capital one of the
most majestic cities of the age. Architects, artists and
masons were brought from across the empire to build

Samarkand. It became a fusion of Persian artistry,
Islamic elements and influences which had swept in
with the Mongol hordes.

The Bibi-Khanum Mosque is one of the most colossal
monuments in the Islamic world. Tamerlane's
mausoleum, the Gur-i Amir, is recognised
internationally as a great architectural treasure.
Perfectly proportioned Registan Square, with its vast,
intricately patterned facades, is one of the world's
finest examples of urban design.

But you leave Samarkand remembering its great
domes. They range in colour from light turquoise to
deep blue and they gleam in the sun as they hover over
the city.

All this grandeur was designed to consolidate
Tamerlane's rule. Now it has a new role. It's playing a
part in newly independent Uzbekistan's efforts to
forge a national identity.

Ethnic Uzbeks have peopled the area roughly between
the Aral Sea and Afghanistan for centuries. But until
independence two years ago, Uzbekistan never existed
as an independent nation. Its borders were only
defined for the first time during Stalin's rule, when it
was declared a Soviet republic. The Uzbek government
is eager to build a sense of nationhood as quickly as

possible. Much is being made of the achievements of the region's people long before the Soviet period. Of course the treasures of Samarkand are fine examples of the gloriousness of the distant past.

Restoration of the city's architectural legacy has been going on for decades. But during the chaotic final years of the Soviet empire, the work was allowed practically to grind to a halt. Now though, the restoration effort is forging ahead again. It's getting faster and faster as the government makes available increasing amounts of money, in spite of Uzbekistan's economic woes.

Those overseeing the restoration admit to worrying about the pace of work being urged by the authorities. They say the government's demands sometimes make it difficult to take the care the job requires.

Aside from being part of the nation-building process, this effort is aimed at making the most of Samarkand as a tourist attraction. There's a huge potential that at the moment is barely being tapped. Go to the city now and you almost feel you've got Samarkand to yourself. You can sit practically alone in Registan Square and watch the last rays of the sun glance off the domes. Wander down the street of tombs at Shahi Zinda and, aside from the occasional pilgrim, you're likely to be the only visitor. Only the wind and the nesting doves break the silence.

Uzbekistan's legions of bureaucrats are formidable. With their demands for letters and form-filling and numerous visas they'll inadvertently keep tourists at bay for a time. But this may change.

At Shahi Zinda at the moment there is just one man selling earrings and other nick-nacks of dubious antiquity. There's nobody around to buy his wares, but he surely hopes that the tourists will eventually come, and possibly in large numbers. If that's the case, the present tranquillity of Shahi Zinda will become just another of Samarkand's memories.

CENTRAL ASIAN EXODUS

Every day, hundreds of ethnic Russians were gathering at the gates of the Russian embassy in Tashkent, the capital of the Central Asian republic of Uzbekistan. They were queuing for documents that would enable them to leave for Russia. Many were the descendants of settlers who came there during the long periods of Czarist and then Soviet rule in Central Asia. But republics like Uzbekistan, Kazakhstan and Tajikistan had become independent, and Russians, along with communities of ethnic Germans, Jews and others that made up Central Asia's cosmopolitan population, were leaving. Their departure was changing the character of the region.
(7 December 1994)

STALIN'S OFFICIALS CAME for Valodia Gelhorn and his family in the summer of 1941. Valodia was part of the large ethnic German community which had long prospered in Russia on the banks of the River Volga. But that summer, Hitler's armies were pouring across Ukraine. The Volga Germans were deported en masse to the east, far from the battlefronts. Valodia endured two winters in a Siberian labour camp.

Later he went south to join his father and hundreds of thousands of other Volga Germans who had been packed aboard trains and despatched to Central Asia. With them had come Tartars from the Crimea, Chechens, Meskhetian Turks and Greeks from the Caucasus. From the other direction, from the Soviet Far East, came ethnic Koreans. Stalin had seen them all as potential collaborators with either Hitler or the Japanese. These were the so-called 'punished peoples', banished to the steppe and mountain wastes of Central Asia. It was a region that the Czar, and after him the Bolsheviks, had traditionally regarded as a place of exile.

But this volatile area also drew some of the most trusted Czarist officers. With them came Russia's finest pioneering stock to help consolidate the empire's southern extremities. After the revolution there was an influx of Russian teachers, doctors, engineers and others to help build the planned Soviet utopia.

Now the outsiders are leaving. They're going partly because it's now become much easier to go. The old emigration restrictions collapsed with the Soviet Union. But along with the independence of the Central Asian republics has also come economic crisis. The handouts from Moscow have ended; the easy, inter-Soviet trade links have been shattered. In some places wages haven't been paid for several months. The struggle to survive is so draining that many people here look back on the Brezhnev era as something of an economic golden age.

Valodia Gelhorn, the Volga German veteran of the Siberian camps, is now seventy-one. In his cottage not far from the Kyrgyz capital, Bishkek, he's preparing to leave for Germany in the next few weeks. His Kyrgyz state pension is the equivalent of just a few pounds a month. Only enough, he says, for two trips to the market. Life would be impossible without the support of his daughter. But he says he has to find a way to stop being a burden on her. Valodia is sure that however difficult for an old man the move to Germany might be, life will be better there than in Kyrgyzstan.

But economic hardship is not all that's driving away the European settlers. With independence has come the rise of national feeling among the indigenous peoples – the Uzbeks, Kazakhs, Tajiks and others. Local cultures are coming far more to the fore. Indigenous languages are being promoted.

In the years to come a thorough knowledge of Uzbek, for example, will be a prerequisite for many jobs in Uzbekistan. Very few of the region's Europeans know more than a few words of the local, Turkic-based languages. They feel increasingly discriminated against at work and elsewhere. They believe they're becoming second-class citizens in lands that they've regarded as home for generations. They see no future for their children in Central Asia.

Struggling young republics like Kyrgyzstan can ill afford to lose the European communities that form the backbone of their skilled and managerial classes. Kyrgyz leaders are trying hard to persuade these groups to stay. But there's little chance of even slowing the rate of departure. About two-thirds of Kyrgyzstan's Germans have gone already. The community is expected practically to disappear. Another 200,000

Germans have left neighbouring Kazakhstan. Five hundred Jews leave Uzbekistan every month for New York and Tel Aviv.

The tide of history that swept Europeans into Central Asia turned with the collapse of the Soviet Union. And the great exodus of the Russians, Germans, Jews and others is speeding the region's return to its Asian roots.

TURKMENISTAN'S EQUINE DIPLOMACY

Officials in the former Soviet Central Asian republic of Turkmenistan launched a special programme to ensure the future of the Akhal Teke breed of horse. This magnificent creature, once the pride of the Turkmen nation, had been neglected and went into serious decline during the Soviet period. But now, it was beginning to flourish again and was symbolic of a wider, post-Soviet renaissance of Turkmen culture. (28 December 1994)

CENTRAL ASIA IS CLASSIC HORSE country. From
Mongolia through to the shores of the Caspian Sea lie
the steppe lands, a great rolling expanse of grassland.
It was here that man first learnt to ride. Later, the
steppe peoples invented the stirrup, which made it
easier to wield weapons as they rode. They became
formidable warriors. Waves of them, the Huns, Turks
and others, galloped out of the steppes to ravage the
settled peoples of Europe and the Middle East.

Horses are still widely used for transport in rural
Central Asia and retain a place in the affections of the
region's formerly nomadic peoples like the Kazakhs
and Kyrgyz. But the Turkmen go furthest in their
veneration of the horse. Their republic on the
Caspian's eastern shore is home to the Akhal Teke
breed. It's said to have been raised in the Turkmen
oases for 3,000 years. It's adapted completely to the
harsh desert conditions and has tremendous
endurance. Turkmen tell you of its extraordinary
speed. They say the Akhal Teke, with its gleaming,
golden-brown coat, is among the ancestors of today's

finest Western racehorses. They tell you that flashing across the desert on an Akhal Teke is like riding a great bird.

The horses are the pride of the nation. A rearing Akhal Teke is depicted on Turkmenistan's banknotes and its image is at the centre of the republican seal. But comparatively recently the breed was in decline. During the Soviet decades there was little attempt to care for the purity of the Akhal Teke and the strain became diluted through mating with lesser breeds. The Soviets worried more about ensuring a supply of horse meat than protecting equine bloodlines. Some Akhal Teke were butchered. By the time the Soviet Union collapsed, there were only about 1,000 thoroughbreds left.

Newly independent Turkmenistan moved quickly to protect the Akhal Teke. President Saparmurat Niyazov decreed a series of measures. He imposed a ban on exports of the horses. A programme was set up to boost the numbers of Akhal Teke and improve the breed. A spokesman for the national stud near the capital, Ashgabat, says the number of thoroughbreds has now risen to 3,000. The breed, he says, is in safe hands and exports to wealthy horse-lovers around the world have begun.

The resurgence of the Akhal Teke is part of a much wider renaissance of pride in symbols of Turkmen identity. There have been moves to revive the language, which was completely overshadowed by Russian during the Soviet period. History is being rewritten. Soviet dogma had it that the Turkmen voluntarily joined the Czarist empire. A cultural centre is now being built at Goek Teppe, where more than 14,000 Turkmen were massacred while resisting the Czar's army. All this is part of the government's effort to construct the new state. Before independence the Turkmen never had a conventional country of their own. The republic's borders were only defined for the first time by Soviet map-makers working under Stalin's orders.

At the centre of the nation-building process stands President Saparmurat Niyazov. He's the focus of a personality cult which often takes on absurd proportions. It casts him as a father figure, the official 'First Shepherd' to the once nomadic Turkmen peoples. He clearly sees the elevation of past glories as a means of fostering a sense of national self-worth. The Akhal Teke, the perfect symbol of the new state, has played a part in Turkmenistan's forging of relations with the outside world; horses have been presented to the leaders of Russia, Iran, Turkey, Pakistan and elsewhere.

But Turkmenistan's equine equivalent of China's famous panda diplomacy has not always run smoothly. Mr Niyazov was reported to be disgruntled that an Akhal Teke called Maksad, presented to Britain's John Major, was still mooching about his stable in Ashgabat months later. Flustered British diplomats insisted they weren't looking the gift horse in the mouth. They blamed transport difficulties for the delay in fetching Maksad from the far-off shores of the Caspian.

MONGOLIA'S NOMADIC TRADITION

During the many decades that Mongolia was a Soviet communist satellite state, its history and nomadic traditions were denigrated and distorted. All this ended in 1990 with Mongolia's democratic revolution when the country finally escaped from Moscow's shadow and gained true independence. A huge upsurge of interest in Mongolia's past and traditions followed as Mongolians prepared to celebrate the anniversary of the founding of their capital, Ulan Bator, a city which was in many ways a product of the collision of communism and Mongolia's nomadic traditions. (8 August 1994)

FOR HOURS THE STEPPE LANDS of Mongolia
passed beneath the plane. The great sea of grass below
was almost completely unmarked by man. During the
whole flight, across half the country, I only spotted
two or three roads. I saw one small town. Mongolia is
as big as France, Spain and Germany put together, but
its population is no greater than the size of
Birmingham. From the air you sometimes see tiny,
lonely white dots. They're tents. Nearly half of
Mongolia's people are still nomads. They drift across
the steppe tending herds in a manner little changed
from the days of Genghis Khan. The spirit and
traditions of nomadism have always been at the core of
Mongol life. The city is an alien idea.

It's perhaps little surprise then that Ulan Bator is one
of the world's more unusual capitals. It began more
than 350 years ago as a large nomad encampment. It
shifted many times before establishing itself in the
present site. Into this century it remained a settlement
of tents. The construction of buildings and roads only
really began in earnest in the 1920s, after Mongolia

had become a Soviet satellite state. Ulan Bator – which means 'Red Hero' – was to be a Mongol Moscow from which the country would be transformed along Marxist-Leninist lines. On a huge square in front of Parliament stands an exact replica of Lenin's tomb in Moscow. The Ulan Bator version houses the body of the hero of Mongolia's socialist revolution, Sukhbaatar, often described as the Mongol Lenin.

Each of the city's drab official buildings and shabby apartment blocks has a distinctly Soviet air. It's as if a piece of the Soviet Union has been dumped on to the Mongol steppe. The style and structure of the city symbolises the break with Mongolia's past that the communists wanted. Mongolia was to become a predominantly industrial nation. But in fact, beneath the surface, the city remains intimately linked with the nomad traditions of the surrounding steppe land. They've worked themselves into Ulan Bator's bones – in spite of the communist planners. The city's shanty towns are a prime example. They're huge encampments of round nomad tents, brought in by country people trying their luck in the capital. The round, felt tents, or *gers*, as the Mongols call them, crop up wherever a bit of extra living space is needed. I saw one of them on the roof of a bar and there are other reminders of the old Mongolia on Ulan Bator's streets. There's the occasional horseman. More and more people are now wearing the *delm*, the herdsman's traditional, long felt robe. Goats and the odd cow graze most days near the Parliament.

But it's in the attitude of its people that Ulan Bator has its most intimate link with the countryside. The traditions of nomad life still hold a powerful appeal for many city dwellers. Even the more confirmed urbanites talk with enthusiasm of spending long spells with nomad relatives. Mothers tell you that summers spent in the country make their children strong enough for winter in the city.

I met an elderly couple in a small nomad encampment some 150 miles north of Ulan Bator. They were pensioners like no others I'd ever met. The old man had been an accountant at the circus in the capital. As soon as he retired, he'd left the city. He'd bought a tent and some livestock and taken to the grasslands. Instead of living out their days in a bleak apartment block in Ulan Bator's suburbs, the couple were completely absorbed in the tending of their sheep and goats and in the rhythms of the steppe. Their family in the capital always knows roughly where the camp is and visits often. The grandchildren spend long summer holidays in the complete security of the nomad community. Among the horses, dogs, tents and campfires the family's youngest generation is being introduced to nomad ways. The children could never be conventional city kids. They're no doubt developing the deep affinity with the countryside that so many Ulan Bator people seem to share; a large part of the capital's population remains strongly, emotionally attached to a lifestyle quite different from that going on in the streets of their Soviet-style capital.